Speak Your Way to Cash®

How To Start at the Top of the Speaking Market Instead of Working Your Way Up From the Bottom!

Ashley N. Kirkwood, Esq.

SBN: 978-1-7362299-1-0 (Hardcover)
ISBN: 978-1-7362299-0-3 (Softcover)
ISBN: 978-1-7362299-2-7 (E-Book)
ISBN: 978-1-7362299-5-8 (Audiobook)
Library of Congress Control Number: 2021914810

First printing edition 2021
Speak Your Way To Cash®

P.O. Box 823
Flossmoor, IL 60422
www.speakyourwaytocash.com

Legal Disclaimers

I am to support you in reaching your speaking goals, but your success depends primarily on your own effort, motivation, commitment, and follow-through. I can neither predict nor do I guarantee your success although I hope you reach great success!

Earnings Disclaimer

Any and all earnings, income statements, or examples described throughout this book are only estimates of what might be possible for you now or in the future. That said, I make no assurance as to any particular financial outcome based on the use of this book.

Testimonials

Throughout this book, I tell client stories and other stories from my life. This is for the purpose of illustration only. The testimonials and examples you will read about in this book are of actual clients and the results they personally achieved. The information provided within this book is for general informational and educational purposes only. The author makes no representations or warranties, expressed or implied, about the completeness, accuracy, reliability, suitability, or availability with respect to the information, products, services, or related graphics contained in this book for any purpose. Any use of this information is at your own risk.

No Attorney-Client Privilege

Although I am a lawyer, I am not necessarily your lawyer (absent an agreement to the contrary). Reading this book does not create an attorney-client relationship between us. This book is for educational purposes *only*.

This book is dedicated to my husband, Chris, and my daughter, Christelle! I love you both to the moon and back!

Contents

Introduction

Imagine this: You head to your home office and deliver a 40-minute virtual talk. Two days later, your client mails you a check for $15,000 dollars. Five figures for one speech—not bad, but on your post-event call with your client, you discover they actually need additional workshops and a bit of consulting. You quote your client $125,000 for four additional workshops, an assessment, and two hours of consulting. You show your client how your proprietary framework will help them to change the thought processes and actions of all their employees nationwide. You explain the value of the framework you created and how it will be a great fit for the issues they are having with their employees. About two weeks later, they sign your six-figure speaking contract and pay you a deposit of $25,000 to start the engagement.

Not bad, right? That, in a nutshell, is what I desire for you, the person holding this book. I want you to land five to six-figure speaking contracts that convert into lives changed for your clients and income generated for you.

If this sounds even a teeny bit interesting, keep reading this book. My name is Ashley Kirkwood, and I am the founder of Speak Your Way To Cash®. We're going to take a journey together. I am going to talk to you in plain language and teach you the foundational elements of landing high-paying speaking contracts. I'll share some success stories here too, so you can see that it's possible *for you*! Most importantly, I am going to give you strategies that my clients invest tens of thousands of dollars to learn.

However, here's the deal, and I want you to lean in closely when I tell you this. I need you to take action. After each chapter, there will be an action step that you can take in the "Act Your Way To Cash™" section. That's where I am going to give you strategies that I want you to implement. I'll bring the strategies, and you bring the action, cool?

Let's make sure you're in the right place. If you picked up this book, you're either a speaker with expertise who has no idea how you can Speak Your Way To Cash,® or you are a successful speaker who is sick of attracting clients with a low budget or no budget at all. Is that you? Then, you're in the right place. Pat yourself on the back. You're far ahead of other speakers by picking up this book and investing in your career. Guess what? This is the right book for you.

I've got some more great news for you. You don't need to know CEOs of Fortune 100 companies to make it as a speaker. Not all great speakers are born with a silver spoon in their mouths. Now, this isn't the part of the book where I tell you I had a hard and tragic upbringing. That's not my story. My parents made sure I had what I needed and then some when I was growing up! That said, it wasn't personal connections that grew my speaking career. I was able to build connections organically, and you can too! My law firm and speaking business are successful because of a system I developed to grow my businesses every year. I discovered a path to success that is repeatable. You can implement my system!

Don't worry if you're new to speaking or never have booked a paid speaking engagement previously. This book is still for you. With the Speak Your Way To Cash® system, I literally have seen clients go from booking free or low-paying engagements to securing $20,000+ contracts. It can happen! I'm a firm believer that it can happen *for you*. You don't believe me? You're not ready to flip the page yet. I'll wait. You need to believe that you can book five to six-figure corporate speaking contracts. I believe it, and I'll show you how to do it.

I know this might sound crazy, especially when I tell you that I'm writing this book at the beginning of 2021. The COVID-19 pandemic briefly ended in-person conferences, gatherings, and orientations. At first, *all* paid speaking engagements appeared to be lost forever, but they weren't. My client booked a $20,000 speaking contract during the pandemic. At the beginning of 2021, I was still able to land six-figure corporate contracts, and I was not the only one who was able to do that.

Even though the COVID-19 pandemic shut down in-person events in 2020, more events took their place. The market for virtual events is set to grow by over 20% every year for the next seven years.[1] That means there will be more opportunities for training, recruitment events, and conferences, and all of these opportunities will be online. Virtual events aren't going away even when we all get vaccinated and can travel again. Why is this so important? You have more opportunities than ever to bring *your* expertise to wide audiences in exchange for five or six figures, all while you're sitting at home, and this book will show you how to do it.

Maybe you've already read books or watched webinars from coaches who want to help you take the first step. They tell you that taking $2,000 for your first paid speaking engagement is the goal. They tell you that you need to "work your way up," and it will take years to land the six-figure corporate speaking contract that will support your lifestyle and your financial goals. Some might even say that it's not possible to make six figures from one contract.

That's not what Speak Your Way To Cash® is about.

I've taken courses with those coaches. I've read those books. I took $100 for my first speaking engagement. One hundred dollars! Not four, five, or six figures... I took $100. Even the people who booked me knew my expertise and my story was worth more than $100. They threw me a $75 tip after I was finished speaking. After hours of preparation, studying, and practicing, I walked away with $175. Back in the day, I believed that was enough. Heck, I was excited. Not to mention, that organization received the benefit of my husband's teaching too. He attended the conference with me and ended up co-teaching one of the sessions—he's by far my favorite speaker, so they really won that day! Eventually, I realized that wasn't sustainable. When I came to that realization, I started using the methods I will discuss in this book to land larger speaking contracts, and after some success, I started Speak Your Way To Cash® to help you do the same thing.

What Is Speak Your Way To Cash®?

Today, I speak at colleges, conferences, and corporate events. I've given my signature speech, "The Currency of Confidence®," at corporations and colleges around the country—it's also my TEDx talk. In addition, I run Speak Your Way To Cash®, a business that changes speakers' lives and helps them start at the top of the speaking market instead of working their way up from the bottom. Speak Your Way To Cash® is more than just a book. The full Speak Your Way To Cash® experience includes:

- The Speak Your Way To Cash® podcast, which shares information and interviews with experts in the speaking, sales, and entrepreneurship spaces.
- Speak Your Way To Cash® Live, the #1 event for speakers looking to land larger corporate speaking and consulting contracts.
- A private Facebook group with speakers seeking to land five to six-figure engagements.
- Webinars, eBooks, and other useful tools on specific topics related to speaking and growing your business.
- The Speak Your Way To Cash® course, which includes several modules aimed at helping speakers land one-time speaking contracts with colleges around the United States.
- The Speak Your Way To Cash® Academy, a group coaching program with VIP coaching, monthly Q&A sessions, standard operating procedures (SOPs), templates, activities, and handouts all geared towards helping you land five to six-figure corporate contracts!

Do you think this is a lot? It is, but it all has one goal—to demystify the speaking profession for people like you. Throughout this book, you'll read about clients who were able to land their largest speaking contract, draft their signature speeches, and increase their income significantly in one year or less. More important than just their stories is *how they did it!* After all, you don't want to read a book full of success stories that don't relate to you! You want to know how you can get those results too. Am I right or am I right? I got you covered. This book will cover strategies you can implement to become a success story (and please let me know about those wins)! Are you ready to put in the work and get some results? If so, keep reading!

What's This Book All About?

I have a passion for speaking as do most speakers. However, Speak Your Way To Cash® focuses on the Profit Over Performance™ mindset. It teaches us to avoid getting burned out by engagements that zap our energy and leave us with empty pockets. We know the *value* of sharing our expertise with our clients. We live for those moments on the stage, but we know that if we're not putting in the behind-the-scenes work to profit from that time, we're not getting what we deserve.

In order to have a Profit Over Performance™ mindset, you might need to adjust your thinking. The first section of this book goes over the common fears and objections that speakers have before they start applying what they learned from working with us. I took that $100 because I didn't believe that I should ask for more. Heck, at that time, I didn't even know *how* to ask for more. *"What would I say? To whom would I say it? Should I even get paid for this at all? I mean, after all, they are a nonprofit!"* (*Not all non-profit organizations are underfunded, but that's a different conversation.*) Those are all thoughts that I remember having. I was holding onto *limiting beliefs* that told me I needed to wait around for someone to hand me a five-figure contract.

Speakers enter my programs all the time with these same beliefs. They feel guilty about charging high rates or landing a six-figure contract when they could just do it for free. Don't hold on to these beliefs. The truth is that there's nothing sneaky, wrong, or salacious about being paid for your work. It's perfectly fine. Additionally, there's nothing wrong with being paid for something that may come easily to you. In fact, what comes easily to you might be the very thing that you *should* be paid to do! For many speakers who love speaking, the fact that they love it, and it comes naturally is what makes it hard for them to charge a premium for it. Is that you? You have the ability to book a five-figure engagement tomorrow but not until you have the Profit Over Performance™ mindset.

Once your mind is right, it's time to start applying The P.A.I.D. Method™ to your business. I'm dedicating one section of this book to each of the four elements of this method: Press, Assembly, Invite, and Deliver. Integrating these elements into your business will make you *unstoppable*. The chart below illustrates this method!

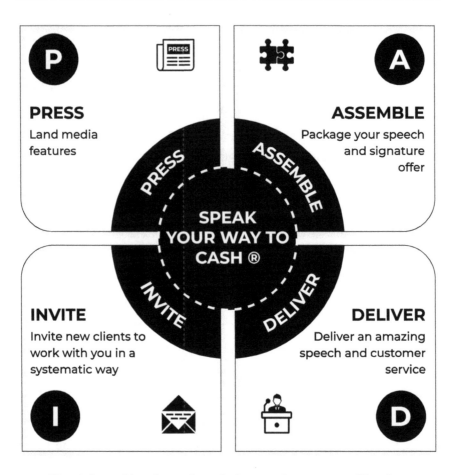

Don't just skim through and choose the one you like the most. You might have a plan in place for one of these elements, but if you're missing out on any of the other elements, you're not going to get the results you want. Of course, because I am also a lawyer (by trade), we will cover some legal tools you'll need to grow your speaking practice and some other strategies I want you to consider after you've mastered the basics. In short, we're going to cover the pieces you need to Speak Your Way To Cash®.

How to Use This Book

Speak Your Way To Cash® isn't about sitting back and letting this information do the work for you. My clients put in the work to get what they want out of their speaking careers. Don't think you can set this book down when you're finished and never look at it again. Don't think you can read this book passively and suddenly have a million dollars in your bank account. That's not how it works. Hopefully, that doesn't shock you. At the end of each chapter, I include action items that can get you working towards the speaking business of your dreams. I'll be telling you to email me and let me know about your progress, and I'm not kidding. Do it. You're not bothering me. You're not going to get spammed. The information I provide to contact me is actually my information! I love getting messages from readers so don't skip those sections. Follow the directions and have some accountability, and you'll be off to a good start.

You already took the first steps in picking up this book and getting this far in the Introduction. Don't stop now. If you want to start landing six-figure contracts, you can, but you've got to put in the work.

You picked up this book because you're ready to do the work. You want to see yourself booking corporate engagements, college engagements, TEDx talks, and more! You want to offer your clients the ultimate solution that they want. You don't want to be overworked and underpaid while doing it. You know you need a six-figure corporate speaking offer, and you're finally ready to create it! You know you should be speaking your way to cash; you just need to know *how* to do it.

What are we waiting for? Let's get started.

Part One

Mindset

Chapter 1

Developing the Mindset of a Highly-Paid Speaker

L et's be real. We know that almost everyone has dealt with self-esteem issues. Studies say that 85% of people deal with some self-esteem issue at some point in their lives.[2] It doesn't matter what race you are, what religion you practice, or how much income you make.

If you picked up this book (and I'm still proud of you for picking up this book, by the way), you probably have experienced doubt or low self-esteem at one point in your life. You thought you weren't worthy. You likely started believing the lies someone else told *you* about *you*. The truth is this; before we can dig into the strategies I teach on how to make money speaking, we have to deal with your mindset.

Why?

Well, it's simple; your actions result from your beliefs. What does this have to do with speaking? Let me make it plain. I could give you all the scripts, templates, and strategies in the world, but if you don't believe it will work for you, you won't pitch a single client. You won't submit a single proposal. You won't do one minute of market research. Your beliefs can for sure tank your bank account, but it's more than that. If you can't see yourself accurately, the energy you will use to promote, pitch, and discuss your world-changing frameworks with clients will be off. You will play small. You will give everyone else's voice more weight than your voice. You will bring that "thank you so much for doing me a favor" energy to every pitch meeting, and that's not going to work.

I am huge on you sitting in your power seat. I *have* to deal with mindset because the vast majority of the speakers I have helped are Black women, and I identify as a Black woman. Here's what that means; it means that I have been subject to images, systems, and studies that promote an inaccurate view of who I am. I have to exude confidence in boardrooms where no one looks like me. I have to break barriers that others wouldn't even see as stumbling blocks. Put simply, I have to fight for my confidence, and maybe you will have to do the same thing. The good news is that confidence isn't something you either have or you don't have. It's something you can develop. I'll share some tips on that a bit later but let's bring it back to what confidence has to do with your speaking business specifically.

You might have told yourself you didn't provide the value that big corporate clients and Ivy League colleges are seeking from speakers. Most speakers only sell to the degree at which they're comfortable buying. I know a lot of speakers who don't feel confident pitching a $20,000 package to a corporate client. Why? They wouldn't spend $20,000 on a speaker for their business. To some, that represents a lot of money, and the question in their mind is, *Who would pay me that?!* Have you ever been there? Have you ever heard people say what they made speaking at a virtual event and said, "*Wow! I could never make that!*" Well, that's what I call divorcing yourself from success! The truth is the first strategy I am going to give you to build confidence is to *stop divorcing yourself from success.* When you see anyone doing something you want to do, I want you to say, "*Wow, if that person can do it, I can do it!*" Find commonality with successful people. I often use this example, and it's a bit dramatic, but it's true. If I wanted to start a large tech company like something that rivaled Facebook, I would look at Mark Zuckerberg and say, "*If he can do it, I can do it.*" Why? Well, we have some commonalities. We're both human. We both bleed red blood. We both attended college, and the list can go on and on. Do you see what I did there? I found commonality with someone that many would think is *"better than them."* Let me be the one to tell you that not a single person walking this planet is better than you. Not one. People just made different decisions. They might have a different path, but you determine your choices. Make choices for which your future will thank you. Reading this book is a good place to start!

In this first chapter, you're going to learn how important it is to be intentional with your thoughts. One of my signature speeches is The Currency of Confidence®. Put simply, to start using The Currency of Confidence®, you need control over three things: your mindset, your beliefs, and your actions. Your thoughts over time contribute to your mindset. Those repeated thoughts that run through your mind after a while cement into your beliefs which inform your actions. Hence, this is the reason I can tell what you believe based on what you do, not what you say. Without the right mindset, you can't implement the strategies discussed in this book. Let's build confidence and convert it into currency, so you can change some lives.

What Are You Worth?

Here's the thing about speaking. I love speaking. Speaking is my passion. I love it when I can walk up on stage, move a crowd, and hear the stories of the lives I changed afterwards. I also love it when I get emails like this one:

Hi Ashley,

My name is Julia, and I am one of the interns participating in the FCB Academy this summer. I wanted to thank you for presenting to us today. I have dealt with the feeling of imposter syndrome for a lot of my life, and this was the first time I had ever been in a space where a group discussed it. It was incredibly helpful to not only hear that I am not alone but also to learn tips for battling it. Your advice on networking was also incredibly helpful—I just created a spreadsheet with my network! I hope you are staying safe! Thank you!

You probably noted the "stay safe" at the end of that email; this was for a presentation that I gave virtually during the pandemic! Guess what? The impact was still there! However, things didn't start out this way. Sure, the income was there (from my day job), but the paycheck from speaking wasn't there. My first paid engagement was for $100, and how much was that tip? (If you answered $75, you read the intro! Pat yourself on the back.) $175 may be low, but free is even lower, and that's where a lot of my engagements stood in the beginning—free. I received no pay, only purpose work. I know some of you are right there—loving how you impact people but wanting the income to back that up! If you're not intentional with your mindset and careful about setting your rate, your wallet is going to hurt.

What mindset do you need? You never can be paid your worth, but your rate is a requirement. Your rate, be it $100, $100,000, or a good meal is not your worth. Your rate is not your worth. Why? Your gifts are worth more than what money can buy. When you equate your rate (what you're paid) to your worth, you'll lack the confidence you need to increase your rate. Allow me to illustrate. If I thought all I was *worth* was what I was paid, I would have thought I was worth that $175 the client paid me. It would have been impossible for me to pitch a proposal for $900,000 or land a multi-six-figure corporate contract. If you struggle to raise your rate, it's likely because you're confusing rate and worth, and believe me, they are two totally different concepts! Even if I'm being paid one million dollars for a speaking engagement, I'm not being paid my worth; I'm just being paid my rate. Do not mistake your rate for your worth.

This is the mindset you need to have if you're going to start speaking your way to serious cash. If you want to have a sustainable speaking business that allows you not only to be well paid but also to pay your team members well, set your children up for success, and invest in other businesses, you need to get into this mindset and set your rates appropriately. Low paying $100—heck, $1,000 engagements are not going to get you far. Your rate is based more on your confidence than competence, in my opinion. I work with brilliant speakers who likely could get clients outstanding results, but when they first come to me, their rates are low. They're highly competent (like you) but lack the confidence to raise their rates. Let's take that concept a step further. When I say they lack confidence, sometimes, confidence is a synonym for information; they lack the *information* to raise their rates! The more good actionable information I have, the more confidence I have to make the right moves in my business. How do you build confidence? You gather information and then commit to taking action.

It's a commitment you have to make, not just to use your gifts, but to position them properly to make the ultimate impact. You have been blessed with a speaking gift that is so powerful, so impactful, and so dynamic that you are not going to discount it by giving it away for free. You can have free resources. You can have a free podcast. You can have free social media content. I've got all that, but you have to set up your business to bring in revenue.

You've got to commit to the mindset shifts we've discussed here. Once you do that, your MBA will fall into place.

The Currency of Confidence®

MBA? No, not like that. When you finish this book, you'll know the steps needed to be able to book six-figure engagements, but I won't be able to send you a diploma with it. My version of an MBA is the degree that no one can take away from you: mindset, beliefs, and actions.

The MBA Framework™

MINDSET — The thoughts you think over time become your beliefs ❶

+

BELIEFS — Your beliefs inform your actions ❷

=

ACTIONS — Your actions dictate your results in life ❸

© 2021 Speak Your Way To Cash ®

If you've seen my signature speech, "The Currency of Confidence®," you know what I'm talking about. If not, Google "The Currency of Confidence® TEDx Ashley Kirkwood" and check out my TEDx talk on this subject.

It all begins with **mindset**. Everything that goes through your mind on a daily basis—all those racing thoughts turn into your mindset. Your mindset then forms your beliefs. Eventually, what you believe determines what actions you take. That's why mindset is the focus of the first chapter of this book! It all starts with the way you think. Let me prove it to you; you picked up this book because you believed it would have some interesting information. Your belief caused you to buy this book. Buying the book was the action, but it wouldn't have occurred without your belief. Now, taking it a step further, the belief wouldn't have formed unless you had some thought at some point in time that speaking was something you wanted to do.

This may seem like a simple example, but here's a takeaway. *They won't buy until you believe.* Before you bought this book, I had to believe I had something to say. I had to believe I had a message. Then, I had to sell that belief to you. If I didn't first believe it, I wouldn't have written the book, and you never could have bought it. It's likely that you haven't even asked a client to spend five or six figures with you—or seven figures, if that's your goal. I can teach you all the strategies in the world, but I can't sell you bottled-up beliefs. You must believe *for yourself* and *in yourself*.

Before you believe, you have to tackle your mindset including your thoughts. What are you thinking about day in and day out? What informs those thoughts or the rate that you set for yourself? You can trace it back to your mindset. What is the reaction you have to a $100, $10,000, or $100,000 price tag?

Studies show that each of us has about 70,000 thoughts in a day. Think about that. 70,000! That's a lot of opportunities to set your mind right or fall into the trap of negative thinking. You either can use those thoughts to remind yourself that your gifts are worth more than what money can buy, or you can fall into the trap of thinking that your rate equals your worth. If you're filling your mind with 70,000 positive thoughts that sound like, *I have unmatched value to give to the marketplace* or *every failure is an opportunity*, you're going to believe those things. However, we're not always thinking 70,000 positive thoughts a day. We let doubts and fears hold us back. If we don't police the 70,000 pieces of information that go through our minds consciously each day, we easily can form a negative mindset.

Write this down: "Everything happens for me, and nothing happens to me." This single mindset shift has transformed the way I move through life. I have agency, authority, and power over my life to change and control my responses to every situation. It doesn't mean I'm perfect, but it does mean that I've determined that every little thing—good or bad—is a gift that I can choose to unwrap and use to serve my future. I don't know what you've been through in your life. You may have had it rough. You still may be having it rough. You may be looking to this book to give you the hope you need to salvage your business before it tanks, but you have to narrate your own story. The stories you tell yourself (your thoughts) about your past and present need to serve your future. Don't be afraid to re-write your narrative.

Let's take it back to business. If you're constantly thinking that your rate should be set at $25,000 for a keynote speech, you eventually will believe it. If you have positive thoughts supporting *why* your rate should be set at $25,000, those beliefs will become stronger. The next chapter is all about the beliefs I have about money. When I share these beliefs with clients, I typically blow their minds. They've set low rates because they believe they had to do that! Not anymore! Remember what I said about confidence and information? The better informed you are, the more confidence you can develop. This book will help you build confidence.

You can tell yourself from sunup to sundown that you believe something, but I won't believe you until I see your beliefs play out in your actions. You believe you should be earning six figures for your speeches? I won't believe it until you start pitching your speaking skills to clients in six-figure proposals.

Mindset. Beliefs. Actions. This MBA is the degree nobody can take away from you. Got it? Your education with Speak Your Way To Cash® *officially* has begun.

What I believe is that you are reading this book for a reason. I believe God has a plan for you. It involves this book. It may or may not involve moving forward in one of my programs or meeting me at an event one day. I am not sure about that, but it's clear that there's a reason you are reading these words and thinking about leveling up as a speaker. Your job is to do something about that. Get your mind right, set your rates, and establish yourself as a highly-paid speaker who brings value to your clients.

Fixing Your Mind First

You control your mindset. You can't control who your parents are, what color your skin is, or where you were raised. However, you can control the opportunities that you see when you think about these things. Even your experiences that feel really cringy or the $100 engagements in the past are opportunities to step up and do something better. You just have to fix your mind first.

While in college, I interned at Philip Morris USA, a large cigarette company. All of the interns came together to do a presentation. We were competing for a full-time job offer to be a sales rep for the company. I wanted that job. The salary was $65,000 right out of college. That was decent money! My manager helped me prepare for the presentation, I was ready to go, and I thought I would do great. I thought I was on my way to big money. Here's the thing I didn't tell you. I was interning at Philip Morris in Champaign, which is a small town in Illinois. However, the presentation wasn't in small-town Champaign. I was competing with a lot of other interns from other offices whom I didn't know.

The company gathered all the interns from around the country to give presentations on how we could make the company better. If you did well, they made a full-time job offer to you. It was just that simple. My colleagues went first; I went towards the end. Right away, I knew I wasn't getting the job. The other interns were far better prepared than me. Their presentations looked better, and they had more data. Their presentations were *way* better than my presentation.

My presentation was just bad. This was my first corporate presentation, and it was so ill-prepared. I'm still embarrassed as I am writing about it! I'm cringing 17 years later. I didn't have the information that I needed, I didn't have the stats. My PowerPoint looked awful, and after seeing everyone else's presentation, I felt like a hot mess. Did I tell you I was the only Black woman intern that summer? I was one of two Black interns *total*.

Here's the lesson I took away from that awful presentation: Never rely on someone else to set your standards and always trust your gut. I relied on a manager who told me I was good to go. She was my superior; obviously, she knew best, right? Wrong. I don't know what her intentions were or if she genuinely thought my presentation was good. It didn't matter then, and it doesn't matter now. Here's why:

The difference between successful people and unsuccessful people is that successful people don't waste their time blaming their actions on other people.

I could have looked at that presentation and blamed my manager for how terribly I performed. Maybe I was angry at my manager at first. I got my act right pretty quickly though. My future did not rest on her motives. My future rested on what I was going to do. Was I going to waste my time worrying about some manager for whom I would never work again? No. I was going to fix my mind, secure my beliefs, and act in a way that would bring me success the next time I had to give a presentation.

The next year, I was an intern at Enterprise. Were you surprised I didn't get the job at Philip Morris? (I didn't get the job at Philip Morris.) I had a similar presentation. This time, I took inventory of what went wrong the previous summer and got my mind right. I was going to have the best presentation in the room, and I wasn't going to make the same mistakes as last year. You know what? I did have the best presentation in the room. I wouldn't have had the best presentation in the room if I had not experienced how embarrassing and horrifying it was to give a terrible presentation. The confidence for year two came from the failure of year one, and that's what ultimately got me the job. Not every presentation you're going to give is great, and not every pitch you give is going to be accepted. What matters is how you move forward, and you need to fix your mind to do that right.

I'm including this story for a few reasons. You have to fix your mindset, take inventory of everything you've learned on your journey, and have the confidence to come back after failure. I really want to revisit the idea that the difference between successful people and unsuccessful people is that successful people don't waste their time blaming other people.

Listen, we've all worked with someone who just wasn't right. I worked with that manager, you might have worked with a bad coach. We've all got a story. Complaining about your old coach or your old manager won't get you any closer to the money. All it's going to do is mess up your mindset! Again, everything happens for you, not to you. When I hire a coach and don't like the coach's approach, I'm thankful because I know exactly what to avoid for my own students.

When you find yourself complaining or making excuses, you have to ask yourself, *What can I do to build my confidence? How can I look at my past in a way that fuels my future?* I tell the story of my embarrassing presentation at Philip Morris because I was able to learn from my experience and build my confidence before my next presentation. I was able to shift my mindset and use my time to serve my future, not to make excuses or complaints.

I did it. I failed, and it didn't kill me. I was able to do even better next year. That's the mindset you have to have if you want to Speak Your Way To Cash®. By the way, I loved Enterprise, and they invited me back to join the company! I still try to rent from Enterprise or National when I can! We all have stories that we don't like to tell about our past. We don't always love to say that we took an engagement for free or that we messed up or whatever. Don't relive these negative stories through the mindset of, "I'm not great," or "I'll never be successful." We all mess up! Your past does not determine who you are, but the way you process it might.

The Wrong Mindset Can Hold You Back From Finding Incredible Success As A Speaker

I don't even know you yet. Well, I may know you, but you get what I mean. Ha. Regardless, I do know one thing about you. You are resilient. If you're reading this close to 2020, you have been through one of the worst years this world has seen in a long time, but you're here. You made the choice to read a book that will allow you to invest in your career and take positive steps toward speaking your way to cash. *That* is resilience.

Mindset isn't fluff. You need it to survive. You would not have gotten through 2020 if you did not fight to survive. You have to fight for the mindset of a highly paid speaker. Fight for the confidence that will help you put together six-figure packages and start getting the results you want out of your speaking career. Fixing your mindset provides the foundation for all of the steps we are going to take throughout this book including every single part of The P.A.I.D. Method™. It's time to tune in to your mindset and Act Your Way to Cash™.

Here are some things to keep in mind from this chapter:
- Your mindset is critical to your success.
- You have to take accountability for your actions.
- Everything happens for you. Nothing happens to you. Believe it!

Act Your Way To Cash™

Okay. You've read some information about the power of mindset, and you have seen your past in a way that will help you Speak Your Way To Cash®. It's time for you to put in the work and develop the language that will solidify your mindset. Write down three affirmations that seal in the mindset of a highly paid speaker. Don't worry if you don't believe them yet. By the end of this book, you'll have the confidence to assemble a six-figure package and pitch it to corporate clients who will benefit from your expertise.

Your affirmations might look like these statements:

"I never can be paid my worth, but I will get my rate."

"I hold the expertise, and therefore, I hold the power."

"I'm okay with losing the wrong clients."

These are mindset shifts that I talk about in Episode 76 of the Speak Your Way To Cash® podcast. Are you interested in diving deeper? Look for Episode 76 entitled, *The Mindset Shift You Need To Make Now To Demand Your Rate.* Let me know what you think!

Your turn:

_____

_____

_____

_____

_____

Chapter 2

Forming the Beliefs Needed to Pitch a Six-Figure Client

Ten years ago, I didn't have a set rate. When someone called me up and asked me to speak for free, I spoke for free. I would take the engagement because I believed I could make an impact on another person's life. My rate wasn't important because I had a full-time job that paid well. I would go onstage, crush it, change people's lives, and make my money from my job.

Today, speaking generates significant income for my company. It's no longer a passion-project. After a while, I realized how important my impact was, and I wanted *this* to be the way that I provided for my family. There was just one problem. I didn't have a set rate! I didn't even know it was possible to have a rate.

A university called me up to speak while I was making this transition to being a full-time speaker. I'll never forget this call. The *first* question they asked me was, "What's your rate?" I was caught off-guard! This was a university that literally could have paid *anything* for me to get up on stage and change the lives of its students. I didn't have an answer for them! I ran through my options, fumbling over what I wanted to tell them, and I landed on a fee of $1,000. Four digits! Reflecting back on this, $1,000 feels crazy. I won't take $1,000 now, and this university could have paid me far more than $1,000.

Maybe you have accepted a $1,000 speaking engagement. Maybe you haven't! Maybe you haven't even taken $100 for your time and effort to get up on stage. I can relate. When I first started speaking, I was just excited to get up on stage. I was excited to make an impact. Having $1,000 in my pocket after making an impact was just a nice bonus.

I didn't set a higher rate because I didn't *believe* that a higher rate was reasonable. I lacked information. My mindset was all wrong! Now, I have set beliefs about speaking *and* about my rate. I know that the university paid far too little for my expertise and my impact. Here's the thing about that university or any client who tried to pay you $1,000 in the past:

If someone can pay you $1,000, there is someone who can pay you $1,000,000.

This is a belief you've got to get in your head as you Speak Your Way To Cash®, so I'm going to write this down again!

If someone can pay you $1,000, there is someone who can pay you $1,000,000.

If someone can pay you $1, someone can pay you $10. If someone can pay you $10, there is someone else who can pay you $10,000. Speak Your Way To Cash® will teach you how to create impact without sacrificing your worth or income. Whether the fee is $20,000, $25,000, or $100,000, you will find clients who will pay your rate consistently.

This starts with reframing your mindset and changing your beliefs to those of a highly paid speaker. You must believe that they exist because they do. I have a college client who needed a quick virtual presentation. The client paid me $12,500 for a 40-minute virtual presentation. Contrast that with my $1,000 client. We will talk about finding and positioning yourself for these opportunities in a later chapter—after we get this mindset piece down!

Successful People Police Their Thoughts

Read that again: Successful people police their thoughts. You already know that we think 70,000 thoughts each day. Repeated thoughts over time become beliefs. What you tell yourself about your rate and your gifts and what you deserve becomes what you *believe* about these things. Are you going to let yourself believe that you are *not* worth $10,000+ for a speaking engagement? If yes, then put this book down right now.

Are you still here? Let's continue.

Policing your thoughts means catching yourself in the moment and replacing negative thoughts with confident beliefs. I know a lot of speakers who come into Speak Your Way To Cash® with negative thoughts about their speaking careers and the way in which they set their rates. They tell me the same things:

- They feel guilty about charging five figures for speaking engagements.

- They don't think that they can live up to the quality that their clients expect from six-figure engagements.

- It's hard for them to even respond to the question, "What's your rate?," with a rate of $25,000 or more.

- They are comparing themselves to other speakers who are charging $500, $1,000, or other lower rates, and they think, "Why would they pay me more?"

- They think that because everyone who approached them has no budget, they aren't worthy of securing clients who have a budget.

I'm going to break a few of these thoughts down and tell you why you need to *replace them* with the beliefs of a highly paid speaker. Once those beliefs are *secured,* pitching a six-figure contract becomes a lot more feasible. However, you have to get your mind right and replace your negative thoughts.

"I feel guilty about charging five figures for a speaking engagement."

Let me tell you a little something about work. I don't *love* to work. I love what I do and have a passion for speaking, but I'm writing this book with a newborn in tow and a husband I love dearly. I'm not leaving them, missing moments with my daughter, and giving up cuddles with my husband to be underpaid, and neither should you!

I love that I can change someone's life through speaking, but I am able to do my best work and serve people at the highest level when I am *well-rested* and *well-paid*. Period. End of story. Wrap it up.

People hear this, and they worry about all the organizations that don't have a $100,000 budget for a speaker. They think about their church or a local networking group. You name it. First of all, if clients do not have the money to pay your rate, they are not the type of clients on which you should base your business model. That's just the truth. Second, I'm not saying that you should never serve the community. Chris, my husband, and I are passionate about serving our community, but that doesn't affect our rate for our for-profit company. One thing we do is tie our philanthropy goals to income targets. Don't forget, you can provide jobs and opportunities when your company is well-funded. We awarded more than 15 contracts to small businesses one year. We paid over twenty people including contractors and employees! That's the impact, but we wouldn't have had that level of impact if we didn't run the business well.

People often say, "You can't pour from an empty cup." I'm going to take this to the next level. In order to serve the communities I want to serve, I need my cup to be overflowing. I want to pour from my overflow, not from my cup at all. I can't walk around with a splash of water in my cup. That leads to burnout, and I can't share my gifts with others properly if I'm burned out. Neither can you. I need to *fill* my cup, and once it's filled, I give the excess to people in my community.

The beautiful thing about Speak Your Way To Cash® is that we focus on processes and rates that help you *fill your cup*. We give you permission to go after what you want. We all have our things, right? Some people have bags, and some people have shoes. I have vacations. I live to travel. We go all out on vacations. Chris and I will drop $30,000 on travel because we make sure to get the best hotels and the best service wherever we go. We also eat well. Don't judge me because "well" doesn't always mean healthy when traveling. That is the way that I fill my cup. Don't trick yourself into thinking that you should be living to work. Fill your cup. Set your rates. Change your own life before you start changing other people's lives!

"I don't think I can live up to the quality that my clients expect from a six-figure speaker."

Not everyone will come right out and say this. I know so many speakers who *think* this, but they won't admit it. This is a deep-seeded, limiting belief that you may not even realize exists. However, that's the thing about beliefs. They make their way so deeply into our minds that we don't even know they're directing each and every action that we take.

For a lot of speakers, identifying this belief is a revelation. I know speakers who have told me they're too busy to pitch every day, or they just can't find the right clients. Some of them say they've been turned down too many times. No! When I hear this, I know that they are not naming their struggles properly. The reason that these speakers are procrastinating or failing to take on challenges is they are intimidated. That's it! Intimidation is holding you back. I discuss this in detail on my podcast. (After you finish this chapter, look up Episode 78: *Overcoming Intimidation To Get What You Want In Life*.)

How do you overcome intimidation and land six-figure contracts? You have to hold onto the belief that *whatever you are paid, you can rise to the rate*. You're probably already there, but I don't know you personally (so I can't say for certain). Take in that thought for a minute. Read it again. *Whatever you are paid, you can rise to the rate*. Later in this book, I will write about delivery and ways that you can put together your signature speech and deliver impeccable service. Right now, you have to focus on that belief. *Whatever you are paid, you can rise to the rate*. Believe that. Feel that in your heart. Say it with me. Whatever *I* am paid, *I* can rise to the rate. You can rise to the rate and deliver a speech that is worth six figures—the service can be worth six figures. *You* are already worth more than money can buy.

Clients are willing to pay $25,000, $50,000, $200,000 for a speaker who will change the lives of their employees and increase their profits. I set up Speak Your Way To Cash® to help you find those clients. I've got that part covered. Your job is to implement these systems in your speaking business.

If you're an expert speaker already, you know that you're providing a service that is worth more than six figures. If you're new to speaking, don't put down this book just yet! Using The F.A.M.E. Method™, you can take the first steps to build a solid brand and carve a place for yourself in the market. We'll worry about that when it's time to *act*. For now, let's secure that belief one more time.

Whatever You Are Paid, You Can Rise to the Rate

"I don't see other speakers charging the rates that I want to charge."

When you are setting your rates, you have to *look up*. This goes back to the idea that you can't sell to the degree at which you're comfortable buying. Holding onto that practice is going to lose you money.

In addition to a speaking business, I founded a law firm: Mobile General Counsel®. I built that firm through speaking engagements. I would book large conferences, stand up in front of crowds of potential clients, and direct them to my business. As I was building my business, I had to set my rates for services such as trademarking. Instead of looking up, I looked to lawyers who were charging $1,000 or $2,000 for a trademark. Everything was small. These lawyers offered one-off services, so I took their lead, and I charged $2,000 for a trademark and hoped for the best.

That wasn't working for me. I didn't mention that before starting Mobile General Counsel®, I worked for a huge law firm that was charging premium prices. Talk about six figures. During my time at that firm, clients invested millions of dollars into their legal protection. I didn't consider this experience when I initially set my rates at Mobile General Counsel®. I was looking at lawyers who were charging what I would pay for a trademark at the time. The lawyers who were charging $1,000 or $2,000 didn't have the same type of legal experience I had. They weren't pitching to the type of clients that I knew I could land because of my experience and my resume. Corporations pay millions in legal fees, but I didn't *believe* I should be charging more than $2,000 because I wasn't looking up to those types of high-paying lawyers; I was looking around. Look up, not around.

What you can see at your level without looking up often won't stretch you to your next level. This is a big mistake. There is nothing wrong with doing market research. I'm a huge proponent of it but don't let your peers' business become your roadmap. Look at the top of the market to compete at the top, not the bottom. When I pitch clients for my law firm, I'm not exclusively pitching to small companies. I'm also pitching to corporations that have grossed millions in revenue. I sell to companies that understand the value of strategic counsel. When I decided to look up and *believe* that those clients were the ones I should be representing, I was able to set my rates appropriately and make a whole lot more money for my firm.

Believe That You Are the CEO Of Your Business

Some of the most common limiting beliefs held among speakers can be knocked down with one major idea. You are the CEO of your business. If you've been a speaker for a long time, this might sound ridiculous. Of course, you're the CEO of your business. You know that! You've been the CEO for quite some time now so let's break this down.

Before you became a CEO, you were an employee. I know I was! I was a well-paid employee at a large law firm, but I was still an employee. Employees live in the fear that if they do something wrong, they get fired. If they go left, their employers will turn them around. This is a *belief* that is instilled in employees from the moment they are hired. What the CEO says goes. They tell us what to do, and they set the vision.

You may struggle pitching to large corporations and talking to CEOs or senior leaders because of intimidation. Not only are we intimidated by the CEO title, but also we are intimidated by what that title represents—*wealth*. If you come from a publicly traded company, you can assume that the CEO is rich. You may assume that senior leaders are paid really well. We are told that money equates to success. We affirm this *belief* largely in part due to years and years of indoctrination from mainstream media namely movies, TV shows, books, and other systems of power. However, here's the thing; that belief is just a belief. You do not have to be intimidated by people, their wealth, or their title. Stop subscribing to the belief that just because someone *has* more than you, that person is more than you. You are worth more than money can buy, remember? We're discussing this because if you keep thinking CEOs and senior leaders of large companies are more valuable than you, you won't pitch them!

If you can stand in front of a Fortune 100 company and help their employees become more confident, productive, collaborative, innovative or all-around better at their job, you should believe that a company has a budget for your training or talk. You may need help packaging your expertise, and we can help with that. First, I want to tell you plainly that there's a market for your gift, and it has real value. Let's just say you have an amazing, well-packaged speech, and the CEO or senior leader rejects it. Guess what happens? You learn, but honestly, who cares! That person is just a CEO, like you. One CEO or senior leader who overlooks your gifts cannot change the fact that you are worth more than money can buy. Another person's belief about your pitch does not change your worth. The rate you offer a client does not change your worth. You are worth more than money can buy. I believe that, and you have to believe that as well. Once you believe that, you can act on it. Here's the lesson. You have to see yourself appropriately before you can position your offer appropriately. See yourself as a CEO, a decision-maker in your company. You are someone with power and authority. Sit in your power seat.

Who Believes in You?

Most of our beliefs—right or wrong—stem from our upbringing or environment. Who believes in you? I personally believe that it can be hard to have an accurate view of your greatness. I set my rates to support my bottom line, lifestyle, and account for the impact I have on the lives of others. Yet, I still put out products and find myself thinking, *Are people really going to buy this?* Even when I don't say this out loud, my husband knows exactly what I'm thinking. When Chris knows I'm releasing a new product, he'll tell me to double the price. Every time, he tells me to double the price, and he's always right. He sees not only greatness in me, but also he sees greatness in what I do. If you do not believe in the greatness of what you do, your clients won't buy what you are selling. Remember, your belief activates buyers. Be careful who you allow to give you advice about your business. They need to believe in you!

Keep these lessons in mind as you move through this book:

- No one is better than you. People just make different choices.

- You can never be paid your worth, only your rate.

- You should never feel guilty about charging your rate. What you do matters, and it has immense value.

Act Your Way To Cash™

Now, it's time for you to speak your rate! I'm serious. Speak it. Say it out loud. Tell it to the person next to you. If you're reading this alone in your house, speak it to yourself. Every day, remind yourself of this rate. You want to fill up your cup and have excess flowing to your community? This should be the rate that will get you there.

While you're speaking your rate, e-mail it to me. I'm serious! Whip out your phone and e-mail me with the subject, "My Rate." Then, in the body of the email, put "My rate is _____." Don't be intimidated! Send me your ideal keynote speaking rate, and we'll take the steps together through this book to ensure that your packaging and your pitch reflect that! Send the email to *ashley@speakyourwaytocash.com*

Chapter 3

Choosing Your Audience

I left a good corporate salary to start Mobile General Counsel® and Speak Your Way To Cash.® I left a *$300,000* annual salary to be exact, plus bonuses. That's a lot of zeros. That is a salary that a lot of people would only *dream* of having, but I left.

Here's what happened. Remember when I said that if people can pay you $1, they can pay you $10? I started thinking about that. Then, I realized, *If they're paying me $300,000, I must be worth millions.* When I took on that belief, it led me to *take action*, so I quit my job. I walked away from making $300,000 a year and guess what? Now, I've pitched $300,000 contracts. That contract may include several workshops and some consulting work, but it's measured and doesn't burn me out. It also allows me to hire a team. Talk about a glow-up!

Before we go any further, I am not saying you have to walk away from your job to start building a professional speaking career. You just read all of this valuable information about mindset and belief. Nothing I have told you is going to make a difference until you put in some action. Confidence is built by actually doing things, not just by thinking about things. You *have* to take action. If you're reading this book on a Tuesday morning, I want you pitching on Tuesday afternoon. I want you to text your friend who works at a company that you want as a client and ask your friend if they know the HR director. That may be a great lead for you, depending on your speaking topic. Ask your friend to make an email introduction. Building confidence comes from your actions. So act! You could send something like this:

Hi Name,

I am currently accepting new corporate clients in my speaking practice. We help companies improve employee productivity through my proprietary method - the AIM Method™. Do you think you could introduce me to your company's HR director or operations director? In the past, I have worked with people in both of those positions to improve employee productivity. What do you think? I am happy to send a sample e-intro you could use to introduce me if that helps. Hope you are well!

Best,

YOUR NAME

All you have to do is copy the above, put it in your voice, and send it to a few of the people you already know!

Getting Started: Selecting Your Expertise

Action is the final piece of The MBA Framework™: mindset, beliefs, and action. Now is your time to put that mindset to work! We're taking *action* in this chapter. You'll want to keep a notebook handy and keep your phone nearby. I've come up with a method that you can use to select your topic. We want to start here because after we know what topic you will be speaking about, we can narrow down an audience for your pitch so let's dive in!

The F.A.M.E. Method™ was created to give you a framework by which to select your speaking topic and audience. You have to know whom you will target and what you will sell them before you start pitching. You will want to have a proprietary method for getting your clients results. That's critical to helping you price outside the market. A bit later, we will discuss your signature speech, signature programming, and framework development, but first, what will be the focus of your speech?

The F in The F.A.M.E. Method™ stands for "Friends and Family." The A stands for "Audience." The M stands for "Monetization," and the E stands for "Expertise or Educational Background!" We will go through each of these one by one below to figure out your starting point in this billion-dollar speaking market! Don't worry if you're new to speaking. The F.A.M.E. Method™ will help to establish your brand and set you up for success as you continue through this book. By the time we get to E, you'll have an idea of *what* packages you can pitch and *where* you can pitch them to land a five to six-figure speaking contract. If you already have established your brand as a speaker, use this as a refresher. Grab that notebook and follow along as we go through each section of The F.A.M.E. Method™.

F: *Friends and Family*

When you put yourself out there as a speaker, I do not recommend you speak on 10+ different topics. It may make sense to you, but it will confuse the market. You want to select a topic that is in alignment with who you are as a person. When people hear your topic, they should not be confused. If you speak about love, be loving. If you speak about confidence, be confident. If you speak about academic success, you should have a track record of academic success. People want to see if your topic is in alignment with who you are. What do your friends and family say about you? Do they say that you're confident, productive, or focused? Do they say that you know how to listen to people with different viewpoints? Do they say that you know how people are feeling just by looking at them?

If several people say the same thing about a soft skill that you possess, that may be a good indicator that you can teach that skill to a corporate or college crowd. For example, I have my Speak Your Way To Cash® Academy students do an exercise in which they make a post on social media that says, "What are the first three words that come to mind when you think of me?" They analyze the responses. Using this method, one of my students, Kelly, discovered that people value her ability to be kind. She then developed an entire signature speech and program on the power of kindness and found that several companies were interested in this offering. Do not undervalue those soft skills that you have mastered. Audiences including corporations and colleges need to teach soft skills to their people.

You should look to your family and friends first because they can provide an accurate representation of your *authentic* skills. If you want to give a speech about empathy but no one you know would describe you as empathetic, then your signature speech isn't going to provide as much value to your audience, and frankly, you may have a hard time selling it because you don't believe in it because it's not aligned. Save yourself the hard work of becoming an expert in something in which you're not an expert. Package and sell the gifts that *you* uniquely and authentically can give to the world. Your gifts are worth more than money can buy so sell those and add tax!

A: Where is the audience who can pay you?

Your message can help you transform lives, but are those lives going to pay you five or six figures? Unlocking the right audience will direct you toward the organizations, groups, and institutions with the budgets for your services. You might want to teach college students how to have healthy romantic relationships. That's great! There's just one problem. Not many college students have $100,000 for your services. Instead, you may want to pitch your services to colleges that host workshops or events. A large, publicly funded, state university is more likely to afford your rate than a group of students. One key thing to note is that *your audience is not always your buyer*. Do not conflate the two.

My clients are typically *corporations and colleges,* but you also can pitch associations and *government entities.* The key is after choosing your topic, you have to then ask yourself, *Where is the audience that can afford to pay me for what I teach, and more importantly, why would they pay me? What problem does my speech or program solve for them?* I will share with you a few tips about audiences:

- **Colleges:** There are various departments within a college that may have a budget for speakers. Schools with more established alumni often have a harder time paying speakers that are not famous in their own right. If you want to work with the Ivy League schools, pitch curriculum development instead of just a one time speech. On what topic can you create a pop up course? On what topic are you an expert? Is there a hot topic that the college wants to feature about which you could develop a curriculum? Also, I have enjoyed working with large public schools that have multiple campuses. There is a lot of collaboration that takes place, and once you are in as a vendor (fancy way of saying a business the college pays to provide a service), it is a lot easier to continue working within the system.
- **Corporations:** This is a huge audience. Companies that have between 50 and 100 employees are a great market. They are big enough to have a budget but small enough that they don't have an in-house training team. Also, you may be able to pitch directly to the CEO or another member of the board to bring in your services. These companies may be fast-growing, so you need to know how your topic will increase their bottom line, whether it be sales or employee retention (it's expensive to replace team members).

- **Nonprofits:** If you are going to focus on nonprofits, look at foundations. These are the organizations that give money to other nonprofits. Sometimes, they have a large professional development budget. Otherwise, go nationally. Look at large nonprofits that need programs that will impact all their local offices. Be wary of targeting small local nonprofits if your goal is to pitch larger contracts. I love giving back, but I do not sell to the organizations to whom I give back.

Here's a visual representation of some things to consider when selecting your audience. The infographic below focuses on colleges and corporations. Some of these considerations will vary based upon your topic, but the infographic below should help you start to think through your selection.

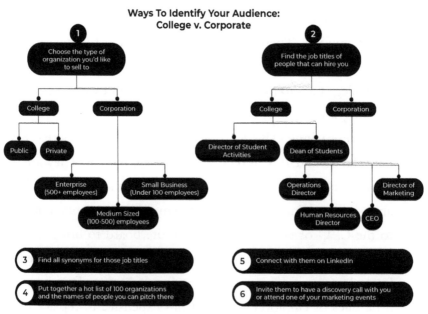

© 2021 Speak Your Way To Cash ®

M: What are the ways that you can monetize your message?

I'm a speaker, but that's not all I do. Speak Your Way To Cash® isn't just a book. If you want more information, I've got a podcast, a course, and a group coaching program that gives speakers VIP treatment as they build their careers. If you go to ashleynicolekirkwood.shop, you can buy additional trainings and products. If you want to reach your revenue goals, you want to consider all the ways that you can serve your audience around one central theme. Not every organization can afford to bring you in to speak in person, but you can license them an on-demand course for their students or employees. What about a book? Think of all the ways you can take your central message and repackage it. Once you establish your audience and message, you need a plan for monetizing your message.

Here are some ideas on ways you can further monetize your speech:

- *Keynote Presentation* - This one is simple. You get paid to deliver a keynote speech. It's typically centered around a big idea to a diverse audience. It is more inspirational, and less teaching is involved, but there are always exceptions. Keynote presentations are typically less than one hour.

- *Workshop Presentation* - During a workshop-style talk, there is typically more teaching and instruction involved and may include a workbook or some other guide your audience can use to have a deeper relationship with the material. These can be 60-90 minutes, but they are typically longer than a key-note. This may be different in some cases.

- ***On-Demand Course*** - You can sell a company access to an online on-demand course that you've created. This is a way to get passive income from corporate clients. You can license access to the course per employee or student, or you can choose to provide them access to licenses in a number of other creative ways.

- ***Workbooks*** - If you have a digital workbook, make it an upsell for your workshop. Don't just include it automatically. It's a valuable asset that should be purchased or used as a bonus to close the deal when a client needs a little incentive.

- ***Train The Trainer Workshops*** - You can sell a service commonly referred to as "instructional design." You would create a training and a facilitator's guide, and you would provide the company with clear directions on how to present the training you created themselves. You design the training. They decide who, internally, will present the information. You can charge a separate fee to deliver the actual training. Be sure to have the option for them to buy a non-exclusive license to the training materials you've created. That's a fancy way of saying they can buy the rights to deliver your training, but they aren't the only ones who have the right to use the material that you created. Exclusivity costs more. Leverage your intellectual property (commonly referred to as IP). It's the main thing you have as a service provider.

- ***Corporate Consulting*** - A consultant goes into an organization and gives advice and insight into problems that organization is having. I do flat-fee corporate consulting, not hourly fees. However, there are a lot of services that can fall under this umbrella.

- ***Executive Roundtables*** - At an executive round table, you help facilitate a discussion around a topic that is important to key decision makers. It can be an internal tool (inside one company) or an external tool (a round table where executives from various companies are present).

- ***Executive Coaching*** - You can sell flat-fee or hourly rate packages to coach key decision makers at an organization. You can sell a bundle of hours that the company can decide to use at their leisure. However, you want to be clear in your contract about when they need to use these hours and how they should use them.

- ***Office Hours*** - You can sell office hours to a company. For example, you could spend every first Tuesday of the month on-site at the company and give any employee the opportunity to schedule a meeting with you during your dedicated "office hours."

- ***Licensing Of Past Speeches*** - You can sell 30, 60, 90, 120, or 365-day licenses to your client. For example, if you do a live training, but the company wants to replay that training over, and over, and over again to their employees, how will you get paid? You won't get paid unless you license the rights to the training to that organization. To do this, you need to make sure you retain ownership of the rights to your presentation and all materials you created. Again, your IP is your meal ticket. Keep ownership over it.

There are plenty of ways to monetize your message. You just need to (1) get clear on the topic; (2) get clear on the audience; and (3) know exactly what makes you different from any other speaker in the world. It's likely going to be your framework! We will talk more on that a bit later.

E: Expertise (or Experience)

Now, what *exactly* are you going to tell your audience through your speeches, podcast episodes, and courses? It all comes down to your expertise. I also use the term *experience* when talking about this portion of The F.A.M.E. Method™. What is your expertise? Don't rush through this section. Your expertise has to be *crystal clear*, so you can quickly communicate what you offer your clients.

Here are some questions I want you to ask yourself when you are trying to figure out what your topic should be:

- If I could give a speech to everyone in the world on one topic, what would I want the world to hear from me?
- What's the one topic that I know like the back of my hand?

People often undervalue this, but this is likely a soft skill. It is something that will change people's minds and resonate in their hearts. Think broadly. Is it leadership? Confidence? Empathy? Listening? Resilience?

If you were handed the global mic and knew everyone would hear you, what would you say? There are two places that you can examine that might inform your answer—your education and your experiences. Think about it. In what field is your degree? What was your major in college? Did you study social science? Do you have an innate ability to decipher human behavior? Did you study math? Are you analytical and organized? Would that lens help inform your productivity training? What experiences have you had? Have you failed 10 times before succeeding in your field? Have you managed over 500 people across the span of your career? Have you helped every company where you've worked make more money? Are you exceptional at sales? Are you great at communication?

You need to think holistically about both your education and your experience. Then, do a brain dump on some topics about which you could speak! Colleges love topics such as communication, healthy dating, resilience, confidence, first-generation college success, academic success, student leadership, and so much more. Head to any website featuring college speakers and browse the topics there for ideas. Do the same for corporate speakers and see the topics companies buy. Wellness is super hot but don't chase trends. Sell the topic *you need to give the world* because it's valuable and authentic to you. Understand that not every topic will work. The packaging of your expertise is critical. For now, let's choose your speaking topic.

Understanding this element of The F.A.M.E. Method™ will help you build your signature speech, develop the language you will use in your marketing materials, *and* write pitches. Have you written all of this down in your notebook? Do you have a better understanding of *where* you want to pitch your speech and *what* you can deliver to your audience? Good. No? I can wait. You're going to need this as we walk through each step of The P.A.I.D. Method™. Get that notebook out!

Developing Your Framework: Tying It All Together

Okay, after you narrow down your topic, the next big thing you have to do is solidify your framework. This is critical. You need a proprietary framework to sell that five to six-figure speech. Here's what I mean. You want to have a method for what you teach. For example, my trademarked signature speech is The Currency of Confidence®. That's the name of the speech, and often, it is the same name I use for workshops and programs that I deliver. Through this speech, I teach my formula for growing confidence. It's simple. To grow your confidence, you need the right mindset, beliefs and actions. That's my formula for confidence. This three-part framework and all its intricacies are proprietary to me. You've already read all about it in the mindset portion of this book, but now you need to create your own framework.

If you teach student leadership, how will you teach it? What is your formula for great student leaders? For example, you may decide that you have a three-part framework for teaching resilience. Action, Integrity, Motivation—you may call it the AIM Method™; this is the method that you use to teach student leadership. You teach student leaders what actions build trust amongst those they are leading, the value of being integral in how you operate and give feedback, and how to motivate people to get the absolute best out of others. Because you teach the AIM Method™, when you are on a call with a prospective client, you are not selling them just on you. You are selling them on your method. Why? Selling them on the method means that they aren't just looking for a leadership speaker; they want their students to be taught the AIM Method™. Well, who else can teach the AIM Method™? No one but you can teach it. It's your proprietary method. In my group coaching program, the Speak Your Way To Cash® Academy, we go even more deeply into how to develop your framework and more!

Now, it's your turn. You need to start brain-dumping your formula for the topic you're teaching. If you teach leadership, what's your formula for a great leader? If you teach resilience, what's your formula for becoming resilient? This is a critical step because having a proprietary framework that is well developed, researched, and easy to explain will help you to price your services *outside the market*. Simply put, you do not want to be beholden to what other speakers charge. If you want to price your services outside the market, you need a proprietary framework. It is important to note that everything you create from here on out including your press plan, social media plan, pitch plan, and other similar proprietary resources will stem from this framework. Here's a pro tip. If you want to find creative ways to make your framework rhyme or form its own catchy word, brain dump various words that are relevant to your formula and look up synonyms for the words. After you have a good group of synonyms, choose the three or four words that comprise the key parts of your framework. Recall our example above - the AIM Method™.

Never Done It? Do it.

We've covered a lot in this section of the book. We've talked about mindset and the critical importance of your thoughts, beliefs, and actions. You now can select your topic using The F.A.M.E. Method™. You learned to ask the following questions:

- What do friends and family say about me? What soft skills do I have?
- To what audience do I want to speak? Who will be the buyer of my services?
- How will I monetize my message?
- What is my expertise? What is my formula for getting clients results? What is my framework?

It may be new to you to think about your mindset, topic, and framework so strategically, but it's important that you take action and start! When you get up to speak, you'll find yourself in new situations. With the right mindset and solid beliefs, it won't matter if you're up against a challenge you've never faced or speaking to a client you've never pitched. You know that *whatever you are paid, you can rise to the rate.* Your actions will rise to the rate that you are pitching or booking, but you have to *act.*

There are some things that you will not feel confident doing because you haven't done those things previously. That's just life. The day before you gave your first speech, you had never given a speech before. You had never coached anyone the day before you coached your first client. That's just how it works! We are all having new experiences every day. As soon as you lean into an experience, nothing will rock you. I've learned to trust myself and trust my instincts by acting and trying new things.

As we get more into The P.A.I.D. Method™, you'll get templates, tips, and more stories from which you can pull when you encounter new experiences. As you take the journey toward landing five to six-figure speaking contracts, you will have a better sense of what is expected, what is normal, and who else is using this method to get results and build a successful speaking career.

Let's talk about a speaker who is using The F.A.M.E. Method™ and The P.A.I.D. Method™ to get results.

Meet Brittany Sherrell

I'm going to tell you about a woman named Brittany Sherrell. She's a speaker and masterful life coach. She was able to use The F.A.M.E. Method™ and other hot tips from Speak Your Way To Cash® to land her first few four-figure engagements *and* pivot her business toward speaking. This *works,* y'all! Brittany is a speaker and a certified happiness coach. Her services help women achieve their goals in less time, kill self-doubt, and get comfortable with lifelong learning. Most importantly, her brand focuses on productivity. I don't know a single person who doesn't want to be more productive.

Brittany came to me after hearing the Speak Your Way To Cash® podcast. She took the Speak Your Way To Cash® course and became a guest on the podcast as a coaching client. (Check her out on Episode

52.) Throughout the episode, we focused on her biggest challenges, and we helped her gain more clarity on her branding and signature speech. Brittany faced challenges with packaging her offer and knowing how to pitch clients.

One of the things we did was to refine her branding using elements of The F.A.M.E. Method™. Brittany brings a lot of value to her clients, but her expertise needed to be highlighted in a way that would attract corporate clients. She needed a title to brand her as a speaker and let her clients know what she was all about. In the podcast episode, I offered some suggestions for titles such as a productivity expert and productivity powerhouse. These titles had the potential to get a client's attention and communicate Brittany's value clearly. If you don't have a clear title for your brand and your business, get that notebook out again and look over what you've put in the "F" and "E" sections from The F.A.M.E. Method™ portions of this book.

Here's where Brittany really found success after entering the Speak Your Way To Cash® program—and this is important to know as we start to get into the meat and potatoes of the book. This program is not something that takes place over the course of a month. You aren't going to read this book, pitch once or twice, and start landing huge corporate clients. That's not how things work. These are strategies that you can use as you evolve and grow as a speaker, and that's what happened for Brittany.

After the podcast episode, Brittany was able to play around with The F.A.M.E. Method™ and identify the problems her audience wanted her to help them solve. She saw how clients and audiences perceived her message. She learned how to pivot and land on a focus that more accurately described her brand. She speaks about confident leadership. This focus allows her to help people leverage their strengths and show up powerfully. Brittany has a gift for helping people find clarity, increase their confidence, and take powerful action. Through the work she has done with Speak Your Way To Cash®, she uses these gifts to build a successful career and make the impact that she always knew she could make.

With this evolution in mind, Brittany set up systems for pitching that made her more productive and led her to results! Before entering our program, she was sending out 4-5 pitches a month. Now, she's sending 25 pitches *a week*. You read that right—from 4-5 pitches a month to 100 pitches a month. Not only has Brittany pitched her speaking services to companies, but she has also pitched to perform a TEDx talk! In March of 2021, she gave her first TEDx talk entitled, "Visionary Leadership: How to Leverage Disruption to Develop Leaders." Look it up. It's incredible! Go, Brittany!

Brittany is a prime example of how you can elevate and evolve your speaking business through action. She has risen to all of the challenges Speak Your Way To Cash® has to offer—literally! The Pitch to Paid Challenge? She did it. Completing the Speak Your Way To Cash® course and all the challenges in it? She did it, and she got results.

Before Speak Your Way To Cash®, Brittany didn't know there was a space for her to get compensated well for what she enjoys doing. Now, she is pivoting toward speaking to maximize her impact and transform more lives. In addition to her TEDx talk, she landed two four-figure engagements in *the same month,* and this was after the COVID-19 pandemic hit. Take a listen to her podcast episode if you want more details on what actions she took and how she used her expertise to frame and pitch her personal brand. You'll also read more about her wins throughout the book. She's been able to overcome limiting beliefs, leverage systems that helped her expand her reach, and more, and she's not the only one. If you want to get P.A.I.D, let's get to it.

Act and Get P.A.I.D!

We're about to wrap up the section on your mindset, but that doesn't mean you can just put your mindset to the side or fall on old, limiting beliefs. The MBA Framework™ shapes the way you approach every element of The P.A.I.D. Method™. You will need to rely on your mindset and beliefs to act: creating assets, protecting your assets, leveraging them, and negotiating which assets are available in your six-figure offers. Get your mind right *every day.* Evaluate your beliefs *every day.* Most importantly, you have to act *every day.* Brittany acts by pitching to 25 clients a week and using The F.A.M.E. Method™ to build her brand. What will you do?

Below find some key points to take from this chapter:

- It is important to select an audience that has experience paying speakers.

- You want to think about all the ways you can monetize your message when considering what you will offer to clients. Think broadly about how you would like to serve clients.

- You want to select a topic that aligns with your experience or educational background. Your topic should be authentic to you.

- Your path to charging premium prices is your proprietary framework. You have to create a formula that explains how you get your clients results. Be sure to give it a name that you trademark. This is your differentiator.

Act Your Way To Cash™

Mindset shifts don't happen overnight. Getting your MBA right is a lifelong journey. Every day should be a commitment to holding the mindset of a highly-paid speaker and securing your beliefs.

Some of the ways I get my mind right are:

- Listening to inspirational podcasts

- Putting on music to get me hyped up!

- Limiting time on social media

- Riding my Peloton (AshleyNicoleEsq is my screen name - ha!)

- Repeating affirmations

- Meditating

- Praying

- Evaluating my beliefs

Maybe you do these things; maybe you don't do them. The method you choose for getting in the right mindset is up to you. However, you need to do something consciously. Take some deliberate action towards your goals.

Hop onto the Speak Your Way To Cash® Facebook page and tell me your favorite ways to get into the mindset of a highly paid speaker. Are you repeating the affirmations from Chapter 1? Do you have a playlist that gets you in the zone? Share your thoughts with the group. Who knows? Your post could inspire another speaker in the group to act and get P.A.I.D! Then, under that same post, go ahead and let me know your topic and framework too, if you have it ready!

How will you improve your mindset? Write down one thing you will commit to do on the lines below:

_____

_____

_____

_____

_____

Part Two

Press

Chapter 4

Building a Six-Figure Press Plan

Tell me this. Before you picked up this book, did you do any research on me? Maybe you read my bio on the back of the book, saw my headshot, checked out my website, or watched my speaking reel. At the very least, you might have Googled me or checked out my social media profiles. If you did do some research, you're proving *why* it's so important to build a six-figure press plan.

The F.A.M.E. Method™ gives you a framework for identifying your unique value proposition and the audience who will benefit from it. You know you're an expert. Your friends and family know you're an expert, and now, you want the *world* to know you're an expert. You want to walk into any room and be the go-to person in your market.

How are you going to do that if you don't have the *receipts?*

Receipts look like an appearance on the local news as the expert in your field. Receipts look like a testimonial on your website. LinkedIn recommendations, a podcast interview, or a book that shares valuable information to your clients—these are all *receipts* that build your brand. When your clients see this information on your website, they'll see that you are legit and ready to give your signature speech. If you're good enough to appear on the news, write a book, or give your speech on the TEDx stage, then you're good enough for clients.

This is why studies show that press is *three times more valuable than traditional advertising.* You read that right! *Three times.* The bottom line is this. Press helps you solidify your expertise, land corporate speaking contracts, and Speak Your Way To Cash®.

This section of the book will go through everything that you need to build a brand: putting together your brand assets (website, brand guide, etc.), using social media as your *own* form of press, and pitching to media outlets in a way that catches the attention of producers. You don't have a website yet? Don't worry. You haven't pitched to a TV producer yet? It's all good. We're starting at the *very beginning.* Putting together your brand assets is crucial to booking press *and* pitching to six-figure clients.

I remember the first time I was on TV. Motivated by Areva Martin's book, *Make it Rain,* I pitched a local TV show. Before I pitched them, I started watching the show to get familiar with the anchors and the content they talked about on the show. (Thanks Areva!) With that knowledge, I wrote my pitch. "I saw your episode on this topic, and I'd love to talk to your audience on X, Y, and Z."

No response.

I pitched them again. No response. Again. No response.

I pitched them two or three more times, and then I was picked to be the legal correspondent on the show. I was so nervous, y'all. If you dig deeply on YouTube, you'll be able to find my first TV appearance. I already was thrown off because I had to do my *own* hair and makeup before I went on air. It was not like in the movies! No one was waiting to give me a full wardrobe and a makeover!

I was totally nervous, but the segment was fine. Speaking on TV is also different from speaking on a stage. Every point you make has to be quick. The producers need soundbites; if you're not prepared, you'll lose focus and start rambling *fast*. I didn't lose focus. I stayed on topic, and the segment was over in what felt like a few seconds.

Walking away from that interview, I felt a little bit like how I felt after giving my first corporate presentation. I hadn't failed, but I didn't walk away from the segment feeling like I had done my best. I walked off that set and told myself, *"If they have me back, I'm going to have much more fun. I'm going to have my talking points prepared in advance, and I'm going to be their go-to legal expert."* At the time of this appearance, I was promoting my services as an attorney and founder of Mobile General Counsel®. Now, I am typically on-air as a speaker and speaking coach!

After that first "just okay" segment, they had me back, and I did everything I said I was going to do. Since then, they've had me back again and again! One time, when they *wanted* to have me back, I referred them to another legal expert—I was too busy working on other projects, and I was traveling. They had me call in—they didn't want anyone else! The moment when they referred to me as "their station's legal expert, Ashley Kirkwood," I knew I had done what I set out to do.

I want to remind you that this network did not ask me to be on their show. I pitched them. They *rejected* my pitch 10 or 15 times before they finally booked me. When they *were* ready to have me on, I was ready too. When considering press, the P in The P.A.I.D. Method™, many of my speakers believe the press is going to come to *them*. They think, *When the press calls me, I'll do what they need me to do.* That's not always how it works!

If you want to talk about something on the six o'clock news, you have to email the producer of that segment your talking points. Take up space. Carve out your *own* niche. Don't just wait around promising yourself that you'll be excited for the opportunity when it comes along. It won't come along if you're not acting on it! The P in The P.A.I.D. Method™ requires your *active participation*. If you want to Speak Your Way To Cash®, you will have to use the press to build your brand. If you want to build your brand, you have to build a six-figure press plan. Work your way to being your local news station's productivity coach or confidence expert. Be knowledgeable. Be engaging. Improve with every segment you book. This all comes from the mindset of a highly paid speaker who is *looking* for opportunities that will build her brand.

Here we are at the P. Press. The first step in The P.A.I.D. Method™. Building your brand starts *now*.

What Do You Need to Book Press?

Pitching is just one step toward getting your name and brand in the press. However, pitching alone won't seal the deal. When the producers read your pitch, they're going to do a little research. If you provide them with *brand assets,* trust that the producers are going to check them out. If the producers don't get your brand assets but have time to do their own research, they're going to hop right onto Google and figure out what *you* can bring to their viewers.

Make sure your brand assets are *on point*. If you can say that all of these assets deliver a clear, consistent message about your brand and your expertise, you're going to have an easier time booking press engagements and getting your name out there. If not, you've got some work to do. To be honest, I pitch media outlets via email, and I no longer attach a press kit. I did back in the day, but now, I include a link to another relevant feature such as my *Forbes Magazine* article or a link to a recent television feature. If you don't have that, you can include a link to your media kit. This would have a short bio, a link to your website, and information about what makes you unique. It also may showcase other outlets on which you have appeared and your social media handles. Make it interesting but don't think that because you don't have a media kit, you can't land press. A compelling email pitch can help you land press even without a media kit.

Website

When you Google "Ashley Nicole Kirkwood," my website pops up. Granted, my name is not very common, but I've also created a website with *good SEO*. Simply put, SEO, or search engine optimization, is the process of making your site more visible on search engines. Good SEO puts you at the top of search results when clients are looking for you or someone in your field. If you're the "Energy Circle Expert," for example, good SEO will give your website to someone who types "energy circle expert" into Google.

Before I talk about the elements of a solid website, you have to know that websites are always a work in progress. Don't aim for perfection when you are building your website. You will constantly change pages, add logos, and refine your website to reflect your brand and the things that you bring to the table as a speaker. If all you have is a landing page, include your landing page!

If you have a designer on-call or have the time to update your website, make sure you have the following elements:

- Domain name (Register that. You may want to purchase the domain for your legal name.)

- Logo

- Brand colors

- Images and videos of you speaking

- An explanation of your framework

- Biography highlighting your expertise

- Call to action (CTA) button

- Testimonials

Don't reinvent the wheel. Also, you want to put together a brand guide for your website designer. Include your brand colors and the actual numbers associated with your brand colors. All colors have a number affiliated with **them, so the** designer can get the hue right to a tee. Include the fonts you want them to use for headings, a link to a folder with all the images the designer can use, and any other brand elements the designer will need to design the website the way you want it. In terms of aesthetics, especially if you get stuck, you can draw inspiration from speakers or entrepreneurs who inspire you. No copying, though! After all, I am an IP lawyer by trade, so there will be no copying.

Speaker Reel

You're a speaker—now *prove it*. Speaker reels show clients and press outlets *exactly* what you bring to your speaking engagements and media appearances. Guess what? Tons of speakers have added virtual engagements to their speaking reel. All you need is a good videographer and some quality content of your in-person or virtual speeches to create this brand asset.

Make sure you're using a set of clips that show your area of expertise and your presentation style. Do you have a unique sense of humor? Feature it in the speaker reel! Do you reference data, studies, and enlightening research? Don't forget to put it in! Show, don't tell, what makes you *you*. Now, I do not want this to stop you, so here's a tip. If you have a lot of random clips of you speaking but no reel, you can go on Fiverr and find a video editor to combine the footage. It's always better to have high-quality footage, but done is better than perfect! So, let's get it done!

TEDx Talk

Have you done a TEDx talk? If you are pitching a media outlet on a topic on which you've given a TEDx talk, then include a link to it in your pitch! Even a small clip of this type of engagement gives media outlets a taste of your signature speech and shows what you will bring to the table. (If you haven't booked a TEDx talk yet, I got you covered. My online shop has a link to my "How to Land a TEDx Talk" webinar.) Head to AshleyNicoleKirkwood.shop and check it out! You also can include a link to your TEDx talk in your signature. I include my TEDx, "The Currency of Confidence®"" in my email signature, and it has started so many conversations! The goal with a TEDx, like media, is to leverage it to the best of your ability. If you don't, it won't help you! The goal is not just to hit these milestones. Rather, the goal is to leverage them to Speak Your Way To Cash®!

Short Bio & Long Bio

This is your chance to tell media outlets *and* your future clients about you. Who are you? What have you done in your career? Why should a conference or a college book *you* to speak? Call it an "elevator pitch."

Call it a "mission statement." Call it whatever you like. You need to have a short version and a long version that you can put on your website, add to your brand kit, and give your clients.

A short bio should include:

- Credentials

- Notable press appearances

- The audience you help

- How you help your audience

- The name of your signature speech

A long bio should include and expand on everything that you include in your short bio. What makes you a unique speaker? What can you bring to the table? Are there any businesses you own or positions you've held outside of speaking that make your appearance more relevant?

A copywriter can help you write both of these brand assets when you have the cash and time to hire them. In the meantime, you can check out my bio on my website speakyourwaytocash.com or check out the bios of speakers in your niche for some good examples. You want your short bio to be 5-8 sentences max. Another bio to consider is an intro bio. What do you want people to say when they are introducing you before you appear on-air? This should be a one-liner that they can read before you are introduced. For example:

Ashley Kirkwood is an international speaker and author who will be join-ing us to discuss her latest book, Speak Your Way To Cash®.

High-Res Photos

Every amazing speaker needs an incredible photographer. One of the best photographers with whom I have ever worked was Jason McCoy. He shot the image of me that's on the cover of this book. He's so good. I had to have him on the Speak Your Way To Cash® podcast to discuss visual branding. (Check out his episode on the podcast!) You will want a great photographer on your team! High-res photos show whomever you are pitching that you are not playing around. Taking high-res photos for your website is best done with a photographer; however, if you can't afford one yet, then it's as easy as grabbing the latest camera phone, a plain background, and a friend who can hold that phone steady. If you have the time, cash, and ability to do so, hire a professional photographer to take headshots. You'll need high-qual-ity photos not only when you're reaching out to media outlets, but also when a conference needs your headshot for *their* marketing materials.

Social Media Handles

Podcasts, the local news channel, and other media outlets want to attract a wider audience too! If you've got a strong social media fol-lowing that will download your podcast interview or tune into your segment, flaunt that! Include links to all of your social media handles in your email signature for producers to explore. Your social media following could be the make-or-break factor in booking you over an-other speaker.

However, it's not enough to add social media handles to your signature and call it a day. Social media content can be some of the best receipts that you can give a potential client. This is called *owned media*, and we've got a whole section on social posts and owned media that you can use to put *cash in your pocket*. More on that later...

Build Your Press Plan!

My appearance on local news was not the end of my press journey, y'all. I've written opinion pieces for a few business publications. I've made several television appearances on Fox, NBC, and other stations, and I've been featured in *Forbes Magazine*. I've booked a ton of press— all without a publicist.

There are three different types of press that you can use to build your brand as a speaker and start making money:

- Owned media
- Paid media
- Earned media

Owned media, like your own personal blog or webinars, are outlets that you *don't need to pitch!* All you have to do is set them up and add your content, and you've got press that you can use as receipts. **Paid media** works the same way, but you've got to cough up some cash. (Think Facebook ads or notable awards that you pay to apply for or sponsored posts.) In the next two sections, we're going to focus on **owned media** (specifically, your social media profiles) and **earned**

media (television, podcasts, print media—all the sources you'll need to pitch). **Paid media** is covered in some of my group coaching programs like the Speak Your Way To Cash® Academy, but we have so much information to cover in this book that we just don't have room!

All of these media sources can bring in revenue so long as you know how to pitch to the right sources. I can trace five figures of revenue from *one* podcast appearance—$10,000! However, I didn't just pitch to any podcast and passively make $10K. I am strategic about the press to whom I pitch, the press that I feature in my brand kit, and the language that I use to pitch to different media outlets in order to book appearances.

You neither have to post on social media every day nor write an op-ed every month. There are plenty of ways to be featured in the press, and you can choose the outlets that work for *you*. Once you have a team, you can pass off pitching, writing, and building brand assets to contractors or freelancers who can put out content *for you*. Be strategic about your goals regarding the press and the way in which your appearances will solidify you as an expert in your field.

I said this once, and I'm going to say it again. Press helps you solidify your expertise, land six-figure speaking contracts, and Speak Your Way To Cash®. You can start building a process that gets you in the press *today*.

Here are some key things you should remember from this chapter:

- You will want to ensure that you have certain items ready to go before you pitch the press, like your website, biography, high resolution photos, and more!

- Do not get discouraged if you pitch the media and your first pitch does not get picked up.

- Your media features will help to solidify your expertise in the market. Keep that in mind when determining where you seek to be featured.

Act Your Way to Cash™

If you haven't mapped out your brand assets yet, this chapter has a *lot* of homework for you. Take out your notebook and write down a list of brand assets that you need to add to your brand kit *this week*. Write your short and long bio, map out your website, choose your brand colors, gather some high-resolution photos in a shareable folder (I use Google Drive), and update your email signature with social media links and footage of you speaking! You also can head to my store and grab the *Pitch Your Way To Press* E-Book for more media pitching templates and scripts. Visit ashleynicolekirkwood.shop!

Even if you don't have all your brand assets together, it's time to start pitching. I'm serious! Don't worry if your website isn't perfect or if your long bio and short bio don't match. Just start pitching. Introduce yourself to producers. Get your name out there.

It's as easy as looking up journalists or editors at your local paper and getting their email addresses! Plus, after you get a feature in one place, you can flip it into more features by sending this pitch:

Hi [Journalist or Editor]!

My recent [Event/Accomplishment] was featured in [Name of Publication]. I would love to chat with you about the story. I think the readers of the [events/business/community] section of your publication would enjoy learning how to _____, _____, and _____! Can we chat next week about it?

Best,

Your Name

After you've done your pitch, search "Help a Reporter Out" online and sign up to be a source. This resource matches journalists to sources as they put stories together. Reporters want to be matched up with experts in their field. They're looking for you, but they won't know to reach out to you until you take *action*.

Done, done, and done. Keep your laptop open, head to the Speak Your Way To Cash® Facebook Group, and let me know how it's going! Remember, you have to pitch *often* if you want to land a media feature to help you achieve credibility that will catch the attention of your clients.

Chapter 5

Scoring Clients with Social Media and Owned Media

Y ou can 100% use social media to land corporate clients. Most of my clients Google me before we have a consultation. I had a call with a client once, and before I could even start the call, she told me that she'd Googled me, found where I'd spoken in the past, called those schools, and heard great things about me. She signed her contract that same day. A strong online presence will help you close deals. You can achieve a strong online presence by putting out great content on one of the many free social media platforms that we discuss in this chapter. If you choose to do that, know that what you post matters. Let's discuss owned media, which is a term used to describe content that you create and share with the world (e.g, social media posts, blogs, live streams).

Where Are You Posting?

These platforms are opportunities for you to hold live interviews or post other types of content. I use software that allows me to go live on multiple platforms at once. I most frequently use StreamYard, but there are many options available to you. Maybe you have seen these live feeds on LinkedIn, Facebook, YouTube, or Instagram. I'm not saying you have to post on every single social media site every day. You'll wear yourself thin, but developing a system for creating owned media and posting content *starts* with setting up a profile on a platform that aligns with your space. Not all platforms will align with your space, so you have to invest time in exploring the possibilities for establishing your brand and solidifying your position as an expert in your space.

These platforms are just a handful of the possibilities for creating and sharing owned media right from your phone or laptop. Go ahead. Try them out. If you want to see how speakers can use these platforms to further their career, feel free to follow, connect, or take a look at how I'm using social media to elevate Speak Your Way To Cash®.

Facebook

Are you a part of the free Speak Your Way To Cash® Facebook group yet? No? Put down this book and open up your laptop. Speakers like you have gained tons of valuable knowledge, accessed challenges, and connected with other speakers through this Facebook group. Furthermore, you don't just have to join a group or watch a Facebook Live event to gain value from Facebook. Host your own group! Host a live event! You've probably got a Facebook account already—almost three billion people do. Scoring clients through social media isn't just about setting up a profile. Use your profile to elevate your career and establish your brand as a speaker to *everyone you know*. Here are some ways speakers can use Facebook to attract clients:

- Create a Facebook group for your ideal corporate clients - (Ex: HR Professionals Using Empathy, Student Engagement Professionals United, etc.) Note that in the examples provided, I focused on job titles of people who hire speakers. Create a space where your ideal clients can let their hair down, get resources, and engage with you.

- Post articles and information that will be learning opportunities for your ideal client. Share stories that help people learn more about you.

- Do Facebook Live feeds about your framework.

Find me on my Facebook business page, Ashley N. Kirkwood, or you can join my Facebook group called, Speak Your Way To Cash® - The Group For Speakers & Entrepreneurs

Twitter

Twitter is another platform that allows you to take part in conversations with journalists, editors, producers, and thought leaders. If the right people can see that you already are having these conversations and speaking on issues that are relevant to your brand, they will be more likely to have you on their show or interview you for their podcast. Although I have a Twitter account, I am not super active on it. My main platforms are Facebook and Instagram with a side of LinkedIn! Here are some ways speakers can use Twitter to attract clients:

- Opine on popular news stories and discuss how they relate to your expertise.

- Share short quotes or ask questions about a topic to spark conversations.

- Elevate the voices of your clients.

Find me on Twitter: @AshNicoleSpeaks

Instagram

Instagram is taking *over* the social media game. It's growing fast. People aren't just using Instagram to post updates or see how their friends are doing. A large majority (83%) of people use Instagram to discover products and services.[3] I'm talking about the services that you offer clients: free webinars, coaching sessions, your books, your podcast, or you name it. An Instagram post takes a few seconds to write. Here are some ways speakers can use Instagram to attract clients:

- Share video clips of your past speeches.

- Share pictures of you speaking at past events.

- Promote events or webinars that you are hosting for your clients.

- Send your ideal clients voice notes or other direct messages with tips they can use to make their lives better. Customize the messages for a great touch!

Find me on Instagram: @theashleynicoleshow and @speakyourwaytocash

Clubhouse

Clubhouse is the *perfect* social media platform for speakers. Why? All you have to do to start producing content is *speak*. If you have a specific topic that you want to discuss, set up a room and start speaking! If you don't have a speaker reel just yet, record your Clubhouse talks. If you want to hear me drop some more gems on how to Speak Your Way To Cash®, open the app and listen to me speak.

Find me on Clubhouse: @*ashleynicoleesq* and follow the Speak Your Way To Cash® Club for free talks and speaking tips!

TikTok

I'm rarely on TikTok. That's just not for me, but it *could* be a great social media platform for you. Social media gives you the opportunity to *get creative*. TikTok is another social media platform that gives speakers, coaches, and other entrepreneurs a chance to reach clients in creative ways. I'm not telling you to get on TikTok and start dancing for your clients unless that speaks to your brand and supports what you can bring to your audience. Remember, you offer unique gifts and a unique perspective that no one can take away from you. Don't stray away from one social media platform or another if it can help your brand.

LinkedIn

LinkedIn is the most trusted social network in the game.[4] If you want to establish your business and connect with other professionals, you've got to get on LinkedIn. My podcast features multiple episodes about the value of LinkedIn and ways to use content to grow your speaking business. Did you know that LinkedIn Live can generate up to 24 times more comments than pre-recorded videos? That's a big jump in comments.

One of my podcast episodes features Dr. Janice Gassam, a client of mine and a phenomenal public speaker in the diversity and inclusion space. She also crushes the LinkedIn game. Go follow her!

Find me on LinkedIn: Ashley Kirkwood

Meet Dr. Janice Gassam

If there is anyone who knows about scoring clients with social media, it's Dr. Janice Gassam. Dr. Gassam is a diversity and inclusion consultant as well as a professor, writer, and public speaker. She also is a speaker who has landed several five-figure speaking contracts. She's a highly accomplished and sought-after thought leader on equity issues!

Dr. Gassam knows a thing or two about building a six-figure press plan. She has written over 150 articles for *Forbes Magazine*. She is a contributing writer to Fast Company, and she's authored two books. She wrote *Dirty Diversity: A Practical Guide to Foster an Equitable and Inclusive Workplace for All* and *The Pink Elephant: A Practical Guide to Creating an Anti-Racist Organization*. Her podcast, Dirty Diversity, is another source of owned media that she uses to attract clients and solidify her expertise in the diversity and inclusion spaces.

When Dr. Gassam appeared on my podcast, we talked about a lot of things: setting your rate, knowing your worth, and generating leads through her social media profiles. Her first step in using social media to launch her speaking business was to post videos on YouTube. The videos featured her talking about subjects within her brand: race, diversity, and inclusion. She also set up a Twitter, Facebook, and Instagram account to promote her business. However, no social media platform has been as successful as LinkedIn for her. Dr. Gassam gets *a majority of her leads* from LinkedIn.

Let me just tell you how valuable LinkedIn has been to Dr. Gassam's business. She started speaking and writing for *Forbes Magazine because of her LinkedIn profile*. When she wanted to give a TEDx talk, she found and successfully connected with the organizers of a TEDx event *on LinkedIn*. H&M, yes, that H&M, flew her out to Germany to moderate a conference. Where did they find her? You guessed right— *LinkedIn*. There are so many opportunities to pitch, connect, and develop your brand through platforms like LinkedIn.

Now, Dr. Gassam didn't put her name and email on a LinkedIn profile and immediately start getting serious offers from H&M, Venmo, and PayPal. This was a process for her. In her podcast interview, Dr. Gassam told me that she has been working on her profile for over three years. Every time she does a speaking engagement, she posts the highlights on her LinkedIn page. When she writes an article for *Forbes Magazine*, she posts the article on her LinkedIn page. All of her wins go on her LinkedIn page and other social media platforms. She told me that she is her #1 fan and advocate. This is why we started the book with mindset and beliefs. If you are not your #1 fan and advocate, you're going to have a harder time building up your profiles and showing off the *value* that you can provide to your audience. Clients won't know that you wrote a blog post on *Forbes Magazine* or gave a speech at a convention just by visiting your LinkedIn profile. You have to put in the *work* of updating your profile, sharing *your* wins, and positioning your platform in a way that truly displays your expertise.

This process starts with establishing your brand in the ways that we discussed in earlier chapters. Do you have a title that you can put in your LinkedIn header? Can you concisely tell a potential client what you do and what value you provide? Are you paying attention to keywords that a client may use to search for speakers, and are you putting those keywords on your profile? Dr. Gassam dropped some major gems in her podcast interview. You have to listen to it. She is featured on Episode 50: *How Janice Gassam, Ph.D. Used LinkedIn To Write For Forbes and Land High-Visibility Speaking Engagements.* She's actually on the podcast twice!

Because she already had a solid brand, when she came to me to repackage her pricing and speeches, we were able to come up with a fee structure that helped her land one of her first five-figure checks from speaking. It's only been up from there! Check out her other podcast episode, Episode 70!

Thinking Beyond Social Media

One of the topics of conversation in my podcast episode with Dr. Gassam was the etiquette of connecting with people on LinkedIn. Dr. Gassam has written a lot of articles in *Forbes Magazine*, so she has people in her inbox every day asking for a feature. If you're not connecting to people on LinkedIn or other social media platforms, you're probably going to start finding them after you finish this chapter. You have to give something first *before* you ask your connections for favors, interviews, or shout-outs. I don't respond to people on LinkedIn pitching to be on the Speak Your Way To Cash® Podcast who don't have something to offer me or my podcast listeners. I wouldn't do that to them! If someone on LinkedIn offers me insight, research, or something of *value* that I can share with my listeners, then I'm interested.

What's interesting to the people with whom you want to connect on social media? Sometimes, it's more content. If you have a webinar or a blog post on hand to give a connection on LinkedIn, they're more likely to listen to your pitch and learn more about you. When I am connecting with potential corporate clients, I may start the connection with a link to my TEDx talk and ask them if they found it interesting. That's been a way that I've served first and turned a connection into a customer!

Social media is just *one form* of owned media that you can use to solidify your position as an expert. Again, you don't have to put out every single type of content and wear yourself thin, but you can find the types of owned media that provide value to the person on the other end of your pitch (or your larger audience).

What types of owned media am I suggesting? Outside of social media posts, you can create:

- Webinars

- Newsletters

- White papers

- Client case studies

- Blog posts and articles

- Your own podcast or web series

- Online workshops

The possibilities are *endless.*

If you've tuned into the Speak Your Way To Cash® podcast, you might have heard me talk about how I used webinars to attract more corporate clients for my law firm. I put together a webinar that would help HR directors in Illinois better understand changes to policies regarding sexual harassment training. This webinar was a part of the funnel that attracted these clients to the services that my law firm provided. I gave these potential clients something of *value* before they even knew I could provide solutions that they needed. In some cases, those clients didn't know they even needed those solutions! How do you think I found the HR directors who I wanted to pitch?

That's right—LinkedIn. As you start to take advantage of owned media, you will see opportunities to develop a *system* for creating, sharing, and pitching your content in a way that demonstrates your value and connects you with people who later will accept your six-figure packages. The content you use to attract clients will depend on your brand, expertise, and the places where your audience is spending their time online.

Part of the Speak Your Way To Cash® Academy is going through each of these owned media sources and pointing you toward the ones that are relevant to your industry and your space. (We also dive more deeply into landing a TEDx talk, earned media, and paid media.) Share content strategically. Repurpose content. Give your audience enough information to see the value in your services and see that you are worth the five to six-figure rates you have set for yourself.

Think Strategically

If you enjoy interviewing people, consider starting a live interview series. Why? It's one of the many types of media that you can *repurpose* into other types of content. You have to work smarter, not harder. It's like trying to book 100 engagements for $1,000. That's the hardest way to make six figures as a speaker to me. You don't have to stress yourself out with more work! There is no need to reinvent the wheel every time you want to post content. Repurposing and *batching* content is the key to taking advantage of the possibilities of owned media.

Let's say you want to speak at colleges. You decide to do an interview series that is aimed at helping student activities directors plan events that increase student engagement! You reach out to several student activities directors and ask them to be featured in your series. Hopefully, during the interview, you not only ask questions, but also you will offer insight that builds your credibility! You're both dropping gems left and right. What can you do with that content after you wrap?

- Post the content onto your podcast.

- Cut the clip into 20 one-minute videos for LinkedIn, TikTok, or Instagram.

- Send the clips out on your newsletter or email campaigns.

- Create graphics for Instagram, LinkedIn, or Twitter highlighting the gems in the conversation.

- Take out clips of you speaking for your speaker reel.

- Write up a summary of key points for your blog or Medium account.

- Offer your services to your interviewee (that's the money-making move).

Do you see what I'm saying? Work smarter, not harder. One interview, webinar, or Clubhouse conversation can turn into so much content that you can use to elevate your brand, and if you interview potential clients, it can turn into more business. I know I threw a lot of brand assets at you. Content that you produce on media that you own can be used as brand assets. If you can write a killer blog on your website, your SEO will skyrocket. If you can pull quotes from an interview series and repurpose them into social media posts, you can engage your followers and maximize your time using these platforms.

Meet Farah Harris

Once you start browsing through the Speak Your Way To Cash® Facebook group, you'll see that we aren't just a group of random speakers competing against each other. We help each other out, and we're all meant to be working together. There is no better evidence of that than Farah Harris.

Farah Harris is a licensed psychotherapist and the founder of WorkingWell Daily™. She had been listening to my podcast for a year or so when she signed up for the Speak Your Way To Cash® event. Now, Farah signed up for the event *before* the pandemic. We had to shift things around when the COVID-19 pandemic actually hit, so she didn't attend the event until we held it virtually in October. However, if you were to talk to Farah about that time, she would remind you that everything moves with Divine timing.

At the beginning of 2020, Farah was ready to shift into a private practice and really establish a career for herself. This is one of the reasons she made big moves and signed up for the event. She had a list of goals for herself. One of those goals was to land a feature in *Forbes Magazine*. Having that feature on her website and resume was a way for Farah to gain more credibility and connect with the corporations and institutions where she wanted to speak.

This is a story about everything happening by being in the right place at the right time and by taking action when you need to take action. Farah had been in the right place at the right time many times. She had connected with Dr. Janice Gassam back in 2018. Yes, that same Dr. Gassam I introduced to you earlier in this chapter. When I interviewed Dr. Gassam at the Speak Your Way To Cash® event in October, Farah made sure to reconnect with Dr. Gassam and continue building on the relationship they had established over social media.

Here's where Farah really took action. She was thinking strategically. Every time she put out content or gave a presentation, she used that as an opportunity to post on her social media and produce more content. She *knew* that during one of those times, she would capture the attention of someone who would give her that *Forbes Magazine* feature and help her check her goals off her list. Surely enough, Dr. Gassam saw one of Farah's Instagram stories and reached out to her. She asked Farah if she would be open to doing an interview for *Forbes Magazine*.

That one Instagram story wasn't the reason why Farah was featured in *Forbes Magazine*. She thought strategically for years. She touched base with Dr. Gassam frequently. She attended the Speak Your Way To Cash® event and reconnected with her. She was *consistent* with the content that she was sharing. All of that played into a *Forbes Magazine* feature, which gave Farah more opportunities to speak. Clients saw her feature and reached out with invitations of their own. After attending her first Speak Your Way To Cash® event, she landed her first five-figure speaking contract. Check, check, check.

However, I'm not done with this story yet. That one booking or one feature may open the doors for you, but Speak Your Way To Cash® is about committing to consistent action. I know you can do more than just land a feature in *Forbes Magazine* or book a TEDx talk. Farah knew that too. She didn't just want to be featured in *Forbes Magazine*. She wanted to write for Fast Company.

Here's how she was able to do it. She put out a tweet.

I'm not playing with you! She put out a tweet asking to connect with emotional intelligence experts. It was a hot topic at the time, and she put herself out there to join the conversation. Thank goodness she did that. A few people reached out to her. One of them was an editor for Fast Company. Many of the EQ experts who had been working with Fast Company were White males. Farah offered a fresh, diverse take on the subject. The two chatted, and at the time of this publication, Farah is working on her *second* article for Fast Company. Additionally, since she joined Speak Your Way To Cash® Academy, she has made more money in one quarter than she made in an entire year from speaking. Moreover, she has landed her largest engagement to date. She has landed five figures for just one talk. (It was under an hour too!)

Look, I'm not going to tell you that the next tweet you put out is going to be the key to landing a position writing for the publication of your dreams. One Instagram story isn't going to be the only thing that lands you a corporate contract. I know that. You know that, and Farah knows that. That's why she thinks strategically and has a purpose for attending Speak Your Way To Cash® events. Her features in *Forbes Magazine* and *Fast Company* have caught the eye of potential clients. Her next steps require her to send over a proposal and show these potential clients what she is all about. If the client's goals aren't aligned with her goals, she has to step away, or the relationship will be a waste of her time.

We have been working together to perfect her proposal, perfect the offer that she has assembled, and find the clarity most speakers are looking for when they first start their business. One thing I want you to take away from this is that both Farrah and Dr. Gassam have clear expertise and a brand that they have been building for years. This is not an overnight objective. Brand building takes time, but the sooner you start, the better! Yes, a tweet may connect you to an opportunity, or you might find yourself in another random situation in which you can pitch your services. Will you have a proposal ready to send out? Will you know how to communicate your rate, terms, and conditions? Can you get up on stage and give your signature speech at any random opportunity?

If the answer is no, read on.

This is why I put all elements of The P.A.I.D. Method™ in one book. Press is just one *element* that will help you elevate your business and get the results you want. If Farah didn't have her proposal on lock or a signature framework prepared, she might not feel as ready to talk to the clients who find her press features. Follow her on LinkedIn and Instagram at @workingwelldaily. She uses both platforms beautifully.

Meet Theresa Harris

Another client with whom I've enjoyed working is Theresa Harris, the founder and owner of Scholarship Momma®. She is a college financial aid advisor, professional speaker, and a two-time Speak Your Way To Cash® Live event alumna.

When I had Theresa on my podcast, she mentioned that the first thing she did after leaving the live event was to purchase a CRM, Hub-Spot, and build a plan for pitching every day to grow her business. Her biggest takeaway from the event was the importance of implementing a system for pitching media outlets to solidify her brand. All of the information on the Press element of The P.A.I.D. Method™ was extremely helpful to Theresa.

Now, Theresa uses multiple types of press to establish her brand and land speaking engagements. Let's take her podcast as an example. Theresa started the Higher Education Advocates Podcast to connect with stakeholders in the higher education arena. She's learned from my podcast that you have to be strategic with owned media in order to land earned media and paid speaking engagements.

Here's what she did. She reached out to an individual working with a federal program that provides different social services to college students. Theresa has this great platform in her podcast, and she asked this individual to make an appearance on her podcast. He said yes. As it turns out, this individual is also the communications director for the Midwest region of that organization. When his podcast appearance went live, stakeholders at the organization shared her pod-cast on their platforms. Potential clients from all over the Midwest region saw Theresa's podcast because she was strategic about how she went about pitching and connecting to people in her industry.

Theresa knows a thing or two about using owned and earned press to grow a speaking business and career. Speaking is both a way for her to make money *and* a lead generation tool for her consult-ing business. By leveraging what she has learned at Speak Your Way To Cash®, Theresa is exemplifying what it means to use press to get P.A.I.D. You'll hear more about how appearances like this one, com-bined with mindset and other lessons from Speak Your Way To Cash®, have helped Theresa land multiple engagements with big organiza-tions.

We've got a long way to go in this book. We haven't even got-ten to your six-figure offer yet. As we continue to move forward and discuss the different elements of The P.A.I.D. Method™, remember Theresa, Farah and Dr. Gassam. There will be chance connections and Divine moments when you are talking to the right person at the right time. The work that we do throughout this book will give you the tools you need to take advantage of that moment and secure your next large contract.

Here are a few tips to remember from this chapter:

- Social media content is a powerful tool to help your clients learn about what you offer. Use it.

- LinkedIn Is a great place to connect with and engage corporate clients, but there are many social media platforms that could benefit your business.

- Share your wins on social media and have conversations with your audience. My most successful clients use it to share wins. Above all else, be consistent and clear on whichever platform you choose.

Act Your Way to Cash™

Alright. Did you think you could get so much value off of posting on Facebook or having a LinkedIn profile? Now, it's time to get to *work*. You do not have to create content for every single owned media outlet tomorrow. What you can do is start working on your strategy for hosting a live interview series, dropping a podcast, or releasing content that brings value to your audience and gives you something to share with industry professionals with whom you want to connect on LinkedIn.

If you haven't connected with me on LinkedIn, Instagram, or Facebook, get on it. Share your social media handles in the Speak Your Way To Cash® Facebook group too. It's okay if your profiles aren't perfect yet. We're not aiming for perfection, but if you don't start using your social media profiles or your website to produce content, you are missing out on opportunities to maximize the owned media that you can produce *for free*.

Chapter 6

Pitching to Media Outlets - Earned Media

Owned media is easy and free to set up. Earned media is a different story. Earned media is any media outlet owned by another source. Your friend's podcast is earned media. The local news is earned media. *Forbes Magazine, Fortune Magazine,* and *Entrepreneur Magazine* are all *earned media.*

Maybe you want to hire a publicist to land yourself a spot in these media outlets. That's your choice! If you don't *want* to hire a publicist, don't sweat. There are ways to get featured in *Forbes Magazine* without paying a single cent. The key to landing a spot as a contributing writer or a legal expert is *sending the right pitch.*

Yes, you may get offers from podcasters or journalists who *want* to feature you in earned media. That is great if those are reputable outlets. Take the opportunity to be featured on their platforms. Personally, I get invited to be featured more now, but when I was first starting out, I always pitched. I don't want to wait for someone to hand me a television appearance. If I have to pitch every day, I pitch every day. In my early days, I was the one sending the emails. Now, I get an assistant to help me out.

Pitching to media outlets can be its own part-time job, and you won't get results right away. Conducting research and building a list of press contacts takes time but not necessarily a lot of money! My clients tell me that they might book their first appearance a few months after pitching media outlets. Be patient. Every rejected pitch or "no" from a producer will bring you one step closer to that "yes." What are producers going to do if they don't accept your pitch? Are they going to ban you from writing for a magazine ever again? No! However, they *will* learn your name and know more about you than they did before you sent that first pitch. Keep at it.

If you're still reading this book, I know you have the drive to build this system and get yourself in the press. Here's what I'm going to do. I'm going to give you step-by-step tips about how to pitch to earned media *and* keep track of all your pitches. You know by now that you might not get accepted on the first pitch, but you will get accepted on the 5th, 6th, 11th, or 12th pitch. Keep at it. Set up a system and let it work for *you*.

Steps You Need to Pitch to Earned Media

Establish Your Goals

Speakers can use earned media to accomplish one of two goals: generate leads and establish credibility. You probably won't be able to pitch your brand directly on television segments, but sometimes you can. (Check out my feature on FOX32; it was essentially a commercial for Speak Your Way To Cash®!) Podcasts and radio shows give you more opportunities to share your contact information and value propositions with potential clients because they are long-form interviews. Keep this in mind as you look for media outlets to contact and craft your unique pitch.

Collect Your Brand Assets

Is your website right? Do you have social media handles that you can share with media outlets? Your brand assets don't have to be perfect, but the ones that are should be ready to be shared. When someone sees your pitch, they are going to ask about you or search for you, and they want to see receipts. Save your approved headshots in a folder, so you can send them out quickly.

Identify Your Story

You can't get a spot on the news or a podcast if you don't have something interesting to say! If you want to pitch a story, you've got two options. One option is to share your unique take on a relevant story in the news cycle. Later in the chapter, I am going to introduce my client,

Dr. Dominique Pritchett, who is a rockstar at using this approach to land features in international media. The other option is to pitch an *evergreen* story with useful information that is always relevant. Stories on saving money, handling relationship problems, or discovering life "hacks" don't have to be part of the news cycle to appear on a podcast, the news, or other types of earned media.

Find The Right Contact

You've got the pitch. Where are you going to send it? The answer depends on the media outlet. You might be pitching to an editor, a producer, a journalist, or an email specifically for pitching. LinkedIn is a great source for finding the right person to pitch. The "Contact Us" page also works. As you gather this information, keep it on a spreadsheet that you'll use later to follow up or pitch again. I like Google Sheets because I may have an administrative assistant do some research for me, and I easily can see when he or she updated the sheet last!

Check out the infographic on the next page for some ideas.

Press Pitching Process

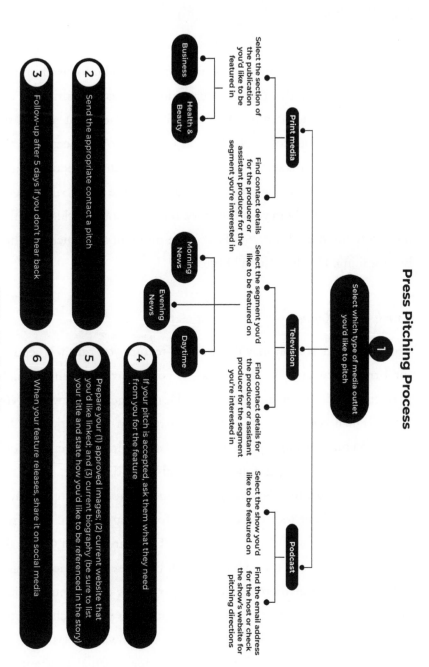

1 Select which type of media outlet you'd like to pitch

Print media
- Business
- Health & Beauty

Select the section of the publication you'd like to be featured in

Find contact details for the producer or assistant producer for the segment you're interested in

Television
- Morning News
- Evening News
- Daytime

Select the segment you'd like to be featured on

Find contact details for the producer or assistant producer for the segment you're interested in

Podcast

Select the show you'd like to be featured on

Find the email address for the host or check the show's website for pitching directions

2 Send the appropriate contact a pitch

3 Follow-up after 5 days if you don't hear back

4 If your pitch is accepted, ask them what they need from you for the feature

5 Prepare your (1) approved images; (2) current website that you'd like linked; and (3) current biography (be sure to list your title and state how you'd like to be referenced in the story)

6 When your feature releases, share it on social media

Send the Pitch!

After you know your goals and choose a contact, it's time to write and send the pitch. Remember, your pitch should be focused on their viewers. Make it about them. Catchy subject lines are critical—"Saw your last tweet and wondered…," "Last night's segment missed this point…," or "Question" are all good examples of subject lines that will grab decision makers' attention and cause them to open the email. Use bullets and keep the pitch focused. You have one goal—to get a feature. Don't tell them your life story, but you should include a link to more information about you! Here's the moment for which you have been waiting. Hit that "send" button!

Track Your Replies

The local news station may not want to feature you on their segment tomorrow. However, in two weeks, it could have a segment that is perfect for your brand and your story. Don't forget to follow up. Now, I send email sequences. That means that when I send out my first batch of emails using a CRM (Client Relationship Management tool), I then send out another follow-up email three days later, and a final follow-up email a few days after that! You have to follow up. Many of the features I have received came from following up three times with the same person until I got a response. There are several CRMs that do this automatically. I use HubSpot, but there are other more cost-effective options out there as well! Keep records of the publications, contacts, and status of every pitch you send. Was your pitch accepted? Did you receive feedback on your pitch? When was the last time you followed up? Update this list *every day* (or get a virtual assistant who can update this for you).

Share The Feature

Once you booked the segment, you're not done. Did you write an article for *Forbes Magazine*? Share it on your LinkedIn and your website. Were you featured on the morning news? Get a video of that segment and put it in your newsletter.

Meet Dr. Dominique Pritchett

If you take away *anything* from this chapter, it should be the importance of having a unique, relevant story that you can pitch strategically to different earned media sources. A producer looking for productivity experts for a segment is not going to accept a pitch from a self-care queen *unless* her story speaks to both self-care and productivity. Radio shows that focus on daily news updates are not going to care about pitches from last year's top stories. During Black History Month, producers and reporters want to see a perspective as it relates to Black history. Identifying your story and perspective, knowing who you want to pitch, and not being *afraid* of using that in your pitch to earned media are keys to getting booked where you want to be featured. This is how speakers like Dr. Janice Gassam, Farah Harris, and Theresa Harris have been able to elevate their careers, and they are not the only ones.

Owned media (like social media platforms) connects us to the press and potential clients. In my case, my social media content connects me to clients who use Speak Your Way To Cash® to get features in large media outlets. That's what happened to Dr. Dominique Pritchett. We connected through social media and immediately clicked. After attending the Speak Your Way To Cash® event, she leveled up her branding and business. I interviewed her on Episode 89 of my podcast. Here's a little taste of what she had to share about her experiences as a speaker.

Dr. Dominique Pritchett is a licensed mental health clinician and a coach to other clinicians. By owning her unique perspective and pitching to media outlets without fear, she was able to make multiple appearances on local and international media outlets. I'm talking about BBC London. I'm talking about *The New York Times.* Yes, *The New York Times.* This woman is a rockstar. Period. She knows how important it is to share her perspective when current events warrant it.

Dr. Dominique owns a private practice in Kenosha, Wisconsin. If you read the news or had a TV in 2020, you probably know what story I'm referencing. A 29-year-old Black man was shot and seriously injured by the police back in August 2020. Every news station was talking about this story and how it related to the racial reckoning happening in our country. Where did Dr. Dominique fit into this equation? Not only is she from Kenosha, but she also has a unique perspective on the case. She is a mental health clinician, and she had so much to offer in terms of the long-term effects of a case like that on mental wellness, both in Kenosha and the Black community at large.

It's not enough that Dr. Dominique identified this unique perspective. She also had to share her perspective and story as a mental health clinician. This is the key to pitching to media outlets. You can't be afraid to go for it. You can't be afraid to pitch. Stories like the one out of Kenosha will not wait for experts to send their pitch. The news cycle moves fast, especially if you're trying to pitch to television. When you pitch your story at the right time, you could end up in international newspapers and on international radio shows like Dr. Dominique. She also landed several large speaking contracts after attending the first-ever Speak Your Way To Cash® Live several years ago. She's been in the Speak Your Way To Cash® family for a while!

Get Your Mind Right Before You Pitch!

Before she invested in her speaking business and appeared in the international press, Dr. Dominique encountered imposter syndrome, as a lot of us do. She felt that she was in her own way. She wasn't sure if she was able to influence others, but influencing people isn't about 100,000 followers and getting free trips to Miami on a hotel's dime. Influence, to Dominique, is about finding the right people who need to hear her messages on mental wellness. She told me in her interview that her goal is to *speak with purpose.* That's what is unique about Speak Your Way To Cash®. I don't expect you to put down this book and book 100 engagements next year for $1,000 each. You don't have to take that approach, and if you *do,* you're putting yourself at risk for burnout, or you may spread yourself too thinly. Speak Your Way To Cash® is all about using press and other elements to set up an effective system for you to work with clients at a rate that supports your mental wellness, your goals, and the lifestyle that you want to lead. Inevitably, I want you to magnify your voice and impact.

Telling people that you have a unique perspective or positioning yourself as an expert in your field can be *scary.* Imposter syndrome may start creeping in. Limiting beliefs may hold you back. You may think that you have to wait for more credibility before reaching out to *The New York Times* or international news stations. Guess what I'm going to tell you? Don't wait! The way that you establish credibility is by going on that morning news show and sharing your opinion about what is going on in your industry. *Your words have weight.* The way that you become a radio station's expert on a topic is by showing up and talking about that topic. *Do the work.* The results may not come through tomorrow but doing the work will set you up to Speak Your Way To Cash®.

This isn't to say that Dr. Dominique is rid of imposter syndrome now and forever. Many of us, including me, will find that it creeps back in when you're heading to a new level in your career! In her interview on the podcast, she made a point to say that fear doesn't go away completely after you book that first press engagement or land a large speaking contract. Confidence is a *muscle.* You have to put in the work to strengthen your confidence. This means shaking yourself off after a news station rejects your pitch. This means pitching *again* or asking for feedback. Confidence comes from consistent action over time. The first few months of building your business are about getting these building blocks together. It builds. All of the work you do and the pitches you make this year will be rewarded next year or the year after that.

Don't wait to pitch, but do not feel frustrated if your pitches are not accepted today or tomorrow. You still have a lot of learning to do before you have The P.A.I.D. Method™ working for you. Remember, P.A.I.D is four letters: P, A, I, and D. We're wrapping up the section with the letter "P." Reaching your business goals requires all four parts, including assembly, invite, and delivery. A *Forbes Magazine* feature won't bring in cash if you don't have a well-assembled offer, aren't inviting people to work with you, or fail to deliver a great speech.

Here are a few things to keep in mind when pitching media outlets:

- You have to find the right contact to pitch. When you are pitching television outlets, you are looking for the producer. For print media outlets, you are looking for the editor or possibly a particular contributing author. For podcasts, it varies, but it may be the show host or its producer.

- When you are pitching media outlets, share your story, but keep your pitch focused on their audience.

- Every pitch should be a gift. Keep it clear, direct, and to the point.

Act Your Way to Cash™

Write out your pitch to *Forbes Magazine*. You read this right! Write it out right now. If *Forbes Magazine* isn't your style, find another magazine. Check out the various sections they offer to their readers and see where your unique story is most relevant. Tell the editor your unique perspective. Maybe you can reach out to a few contributors whose stories resonate with you—you're helping them! They need great content! Follow up. Make a note of where you pitched, who you emailed, and whether they accepted the pitch when you hear back from them. Get started *now*, and BCC me on one of those pitches. I want to hear your story!

Part Three

Assembly

Chapter 7

Understanding the Basics of Sales

B efore we dive into what to put in your proposal, we have to cover the basics of sales!

Assembly is about packaging your speech *and* your signature offer. What are you going to tell the CEO of PepsiCo when he asks you what services you can sell him? If you only offer him a one-hour keynote speech, that's the only service he can buy. If you have a full package with workshops, licensing options, and coaching, the CEO can accept a much better package and put more money in your pocket.

This is where sales come in. Speak Your Way To Cash® is about offering a suite of services based on your framework. People can get tripped up when they start to put these packages together. Once you have the package, you have to sell the package. Even the *thought* of selling a $100,000 or $250,000 package could feel wrong. Don't let it. You have to get in the right mindset before you assemble your offer and then *invite* your clients to accept the offer. To get in the right mindset, we have to talk about the basics of sales.

My background is in sales so let me rewind back a few years. You already know I interned for Philip Morris as an outside sales rep. I also worked at Enterprise doing customer service and sales for a little bit. My inside sales experience took place at a company called Acquirent. Every day, I made 100 sales calls. That's right. When I added it all up, I made more than 20,000 sales calls during my time there. I know a thing or two about how to close clients over the phone. It starts with the right mindset.

The Basics of a Sales Mindset

Every day at Acquirent started the same way. We would gather together for 15 minutes and listen to motivational speakers. We needed to get in the right mindset if we wanted to pick up the phone 100 times and get rejected 95 times. That's right. Of those 100 sales calls, maybe five would buy what I was selling or want to know more. That was okay! I made my sales quota from those five calls.

Now, I don't start my day with a 15-minute huddle. The way I step into the right mindset looks different than it did in my inside sales days. Instead, I repeat affirmations that remind me of who I am, what I do, and how I am helping my clients. I want to share a few affirmations with you along with some stories to remind you that *your gifts are worth more than money can buy*. When you assemble a $100,000 package, you have to remember that you are worth *far more than that*.

Other People Will Buy Into What You Are Selling. Do not forget this! There is always someone who will be willing to buy the package that you have to offer. Money and time may be barriers, but those barriers can be overcome. Keep this idea in mind every time a pitch is not accepted, or you find yourself hitting a wall. Someone out there will say, "Yes."

I talk about this further in my podcast episode, *What I Learned From Doing 20,000 Sales Calls That You Can Apply To Your Business.* People will buy what you are selling. In the worst case scenario, you will close a deal after a few rejections. In the best case scenario, the people who rejected you will *see* that you closed a deal with someone else and find their way back to you in a few months.

Never Give Up Your Power Seat. One of the biggest mistakes that speakers make when they pitch is giving up their power. You are not asking clients to do you a favor. You are asking them to work with you because you have something revolutionary that will help them. Remember that proprietary framework we discussed earlier? That's critical to this. You have to have a product that will help them. If you believe that in your heart, you should have no problem assembling a package that will move their objectives forward. It's about who they are, what they want, and how you can provide it. Be the solution.

How do you stay in your power seat when you're pitching 300 clients a week or making 100 calls a day? You chase the "no." A lot of people in sales chase the "yes." They hope and pray that their first, second, or third pitch is going to result in a sale. That's just not how it works! When I worked for Acquirent, I was told "no" over 90 times a day. I knew that for every 95 people who said "no," five people would say "yes." I would be relieved when I heard "no" from a client. I was that much closer to the "yes." Plus, you can get all types of feedback, contact information, and useful data from the "no." This gives you more power the next time you pick up the phone.

Knowledge is power. Data is power, and knowing the right information can build your confidence. Understanding what your clients want and inviting them to come get what they want through your products and services is power. Also, let me tell you how my speaking career started. For six months straight, I pitched 150 clients a day three times per week. That was how I landed my first six figures in speaking. It was through cold emailing people with job titles who could hire me. More than 90% of the people I emailed never replied or said they weren't interested. I built my career on the 5-7% of people who wanted to do business with me! The mistake that I made early on was only offering them two ways to work with me—through a workshop or a keynote. I didn't have a well-assembled package, and that was a huge mistake. It also was a mistake that I quickly rectified. Three clients easily can represent $300,000 of revenue or more! That's due to proper packaging.

This Is Going to Take Time. Sales is all about relationships. You already have a great service to give to people. Your gifts are worth more than money can buy. The key to getting people to hand over their wallets and buy into six-figure packages is the relationship you build with them. This includes the relationship you build with them *after* their first, second, or third "no."

I told you about the news station that booked me only after I sent 10 pitches. Sales works the same way. Your clients may not have the budget to sign onto your package this year, but they may be ready next year. The people to whom you talk might not have the authority to buy from you, but if you maintain a strong relationship with them, you may be able to get the right contact information and land a six-figure contract. People get promoted, change jobs, and adjust their budgets all the time. None of this happens overnight. The key to landing that six-figure contract, sometimes, is being patient with the people who tell you "no" and maintaining your relationship until they are in a position to tell you "yes." How? Well, remember those assets we talked about you creating in the owned media section of this book? You can send them a newsletter quarterly or see if they want to be added to your mailing list! You can invite them to be on your podcast or share the content they post online. You can send them holiday cards or congratulate them on career milestones. Relationship building is about touchpoints and genuine concern. This is why it's critical that you have a CRM with this information in it!

Selling Is Service

I know a lot of people who hear "no" and walk away. There is so much more you can do before you walk away for good. Not every client is in a position to hand over $180,000 on a package or even $10,000 for one speech. That doesn't mean that they don't need your help. Your gifts are worth more than money can buy. Your clients can benefit from your knowledge, even if it's just the smallest gem that you dropped on an Instagram Live or in a podcast episode. My first six-figure contract came from a client who thought they needed a single talk. They wanted to spend less than $10,000. It wasn't until we had a sales call, and I showed them all the areas in their business that could use our services that they realized they needed more help. If I only had offered them what they believed they needed, I would have lost the opportunity to serve them at a higher level.

Clients may say "no" solely because they do not have the budget for you *yet*. That's okay! When a speaker says they can't afford the Speak Your Way To Cash® Academy, I might direct them to my podcast. Maybe I will send them the link to buy this book. They might not have the budget for the Speak Your Way To Cash® Academy, but they might have the budget for the course. This information is still useful and shows the *value* of what I am selling. People save up money to buy my courses, attend my events, or enroll in the Speak Your Way To Cash® Academy all the time. I know that. I know the content I do offer—podcasts, the Facebook group, and other owned media—is part of the reason that they do commit to the larger sales. If I were to write off every person who said "no" to signing up for the Speak Your Way To Cash® Academy today, I wouldn't have as many students next year.

You need the same mindset when you're selling. *You* are helping your clients, and you care about people, so if they can't invest with you just yet, give them a way to continue learning from you. *You* are helping your clients. Picking up the phone and selling isn't about trying to cheat your clients out of money! They get *value* in what you are offering them. They should be thanking *you* for picking up the phone and offering your knowledge.

Never Feel Bad About Selling. Don't feel guilty about picking up the phone and inviting a client to experience what you have to offer. This ties back into the idea that "selling is service." Clients who accept your offer aren't doing you a favor. They are accepting an invitation from you to add value to their business and their lives. That's why I advocate for value-based pricing. You have an opportunity to serve your clients. You just have to show them what level of service you are willing to provide to them.

If you go to a restaurant, and the menu charges one dollar for a meal, you're going to have low expectations for that meal. If the cost of the meal is $700, you are going to expect a lot more. You might expect better service from the waitstaff. The chefs in the kitchen are likely more invested in bringing you a quality meal. The same principle applies to speaking. Clients are going to expect a high level of service if you're charging six figures. Corporate clients or colleges that are investing in their students only will hire someone who is providing that high level of service.

Remember, I do my best work when I am well-rested and well-paid. I bet you do too. If you are not well-rested and well-paid, you cannot give your gifts to the best of your ability. If you've booked 100 engagements a year, and you're still having trouble paying the mortgage, your audience is not going to get the best version of you.

They're just not! Don't feel bad about selling. The right clients are paying *their* employees six figures without batting an eye. If you come in and tell these clients that you can help them get more value out of each employee without raising their salaries, that client will have no problem handing you six figures too.

Different Types of Selling

I know that you can take on a sales mindset because you're *already doing sales*. We all sell to people *all day long*. Have you convinced your children to eat their vegetables when they are pouting at the table? That is sales. Have you ever asked for a promotion at work? That is sales. Some people say that asking another person out to dinner is sales. You already know how to get another person to cooperate in a transaction. Think of selling your package as *the same thing*.

I want you to focus on specific types of selling that will attract the *right clients* with the *right qualifiers*. You can sell to church groups and sewing circles all day, but they are unlikely to have the budget for a six-figure speaking package. If you've followed me for a long time, you know that my dad is a pastor, and my husband also used to be a pastor at a church, so I have much respect for religious institutions. In my experience, making churches your only audience limits your financial scalability as a speaker! There are always exceptions, but those are my thoughts on that. You need to target the appropriate clients, position your package as the valuable service that it is, and lead them all the way to sign on the dotted line. Now, let me give you a disclaimer. Even when you have a targeted list of clients, they will not all say yes. This is why it is critical to choose a market that is large enough for you to dominate a portion of it and is used to hiring speakers.

You do not want to sell a potential client on the professional speaking/consulting industry as a whole, on your framework, and on you. That's too much work. I focus on colleges. My clients are student activities directors, provosts, and heads of academic departments. I also focus on corporations. My clients there include HR directors, heads of marketing, and heads of sales. As a reminder, you want to develop your own hot list of potential clients whom you can target. Do some research and get all the synonyms for those job titles. Then, you should have a virtual assistant find their contact information and LinkedIn profiles, so you can connect with them. In the "Invite" portion of the book, we will talk about how you can offer them something of value, so your first interaction is a gift rather than an intrusion!

How We Approach Selling at Speak Your Way To Cash®

Salespeople take very different approaches to selling depending on the services they are promoting or the clientele they want to reach. The best salespeople, however, have one thing in common. They have a clear sales process that they follow to discover leads, warm them up, and convert them into paying clients. The next few chapters will start to dive into developing your sales process and putting together a package that you can use when you sell.

At Speak Your Way To Cash®, we focus heavily on outbound marketing and pitching clients directly through cold emailing. We also focus on inviting new clients to work with you by hosting events that allow you to serve them first. These are not the *only* methods of selling, but they are what I have used to grow my businesses, so we will start there. The infographic below includes a few other sales methods to consider:

© 2021 Speak Your Way To Cash ®

Below are a few key points from this chapter that you should not forget:

- Never give up your power seat. You are not begging for anything. You are offering your clients an opportunity to work with you.

- When selling, your worst case scenario is that the client says "no," and that is not that bad. You can overcome objections, but you can't overcome inaction. You have to take action.

Act Your Way to Cash™

Get yourself in a routine of hyping yourself up in the morning. We needed just 15 minutes a day at Acquirent to motivate us to make 100 phone calls. Even if you don't plan to invite a client to work with you tomorrow, start building this routine. Are you going to meditate? Listen to a podcast? Repeat affirmations? Talk about your morning routine in the Speak Your Way To Cash® Facebook group. The ideas you have might inspire other people to elevate their mornings and get in the right mindset to sell.

Chapter 8

Choosing The Services For Your Six-Figure Proposal

I f you attend Speak Your Way To Cash® events, you'll hear me ask one question over and over again. *If you met the CEO of PepsiCo while at the grocery store, and he asked you to pitch your services, would you be ready?*

This sounds like a funny hypothetical scenario, but I've had Speak Your Way To Cash® alumni pitch their services in the most *random* places! Take Dr. Dominique Pritchett. Yes, the same Dr. Dominique who was featured by the international media giant, BBC London. Since attending Speak Your Way To Cash®, she has landed her largest paid speaking engagement to date. You want to know where she landed that engagement? *The airport.*

I'm serious! Dr. Dominique was sitting in the airport when she was approached by a man who heard her speak at another event. They started talking, and he introduced himself as the CEO of a *huge* company. Once she heard that, she knew she had to start her pitch. The CEO said his company was having some issues surrounding anxiety and finances. As a mental health clinician, Dr. Dominique knew that she could provide solutions regarding anxiety. More importantly, she could provide those solutions as part of a *package* that brought her back to the company again and again. Anxiety doesn't go away after one speech! When she pitched the CEO on this package, he was ready to talk about money *and* rates!

Let me ask my question again, but with a twist: *If the CEO of a huge company asked you to pitch your services in the airport, would you be ready?*

Dr. Dominique told me that she lowballed herself in the airport but was offered more money in the final deal. It was her biggest payout to date! Once she realized the value of the contract that she was offered, her mindset shifted. She told me that she realized *you have to show up how you deserve to show up*. This was an amazing win for Dr. Dominique.

Avoiding the Biggest Mistake Made By Speakers

When Dr. Dominique was talking to her client in the airport, she had already been a part of Speak Your Way To Cash®. She knew that she wasn't going to make the *biggest mistake speakers make*—pitching a one-time engagement.

The first time I got paid $1,000 for a speech, my rate was set for a one-time engagement. I did the speech for the client, gathered some testimonials, and went on my way. As I started reading the testimonials, I saw how much the students got from my speech. They said they wished the speech was longer. They wanted more. They said I did such a great job, and they wanted to have me back next year.

Well, dang! I felt so good reading those testimonials. Then, it hit me. I never was going to see those students again! Even if I *did* return to give a similar speech the following year, I wouldn't be able to help make the transformation I *knew* the students could get out of my services. What you have to understand is that at the end of the day, I want to change lives. I got into speaking because I want to change lives, and I know you know that feeling because you probably wouldn't be reading this book if you didn't want to change lives. We know that motivational speaking is an art, but its effect eventually *wears off*. You know that sense of freshness you have when you first get your clothes out of the dryer? They smell so clean, right? That scent is strong at first, but after an hour or two, that smell has worn off. You can't get the freshness anymore. That's what speaking is like. If I wanted the students to get the goodness from my speeches, I would have to revisit them at *least* a few times per year.

When I contacted the client about another engagement, the client gave me a reality check. They told me they *would* have hired me back, but they didn't know what I offered! I only gave the client one solution to the organization's problems—an hour-long keynote speech. Why did I only give the client that one solution? I wanted that check. I was so focused on the $1,000 payment that I forgot my larger goals. I can't change lives with one speech! Sure, I could say something in this book or in my TEDx talk that some people would use to change their lives forever, but if I wanted to be a part of those transformations, I needed to keep coming back. I needed to engage with the people and see them grow.

When you speak for 60 minutes, you may be able to touch on some of the ways that an audience learns and grows, but you won't get the personal feedback that you can use in your next speech or consultation. My group coaching programs have spanned from a few months to one year, and regardless of the length, I have found that spending consistent time with my individual clients helps them stay motivated to make real change. I also am able to track progress and success! It's the same for my larger corporate clients. People are people, and change doesn't happen overnight. If you want to make a change, you need to work with clients on a deeper level. You can automate some of the touchpoints or sell them a pre-recorded training that they can license with consulting call check-ins, but, in many cases, you need more touchpoints to make lasting changes!

Let's go back to the client I fumbled. The client had gone ahead and hired other speakers to speak on topics within my wheelhouse. The client brought in other consultants to handle business topics that I could have covered easily. I could have been the one to be there for the students and teach them, but I wasn't. At first, I felt salty about that. However, I realized that was *my fault*. I didn't ask the client immediately what else the organization needed. I didn't think of pitching a bigger package with multiple speeches and consultations. When I initially pitched the client, I didn't ask the questions required to understand the client's real vision.

Do you want to change the lives of your clients? Of course, you do. That's your job as a transformational speaker. Your job is also to show clients the solution to the problems they vocalize to you. Most of the time, those problems can't be solved in a 60-minute speech. Employees who need help being more productive may need templates and planning sessions in addition to a keynote speech. College students who are searching for jobs may need one-on-one coaching sessions on how to write a great cover letter. There are so many opportunities for you to provide solutions, and you're doing your clients a disservice by not offering them these solutions. What's worse is that you are doing *yourself* a disservice by trying to book 100 engagements for $1,000 each with clients who would be happy to pay you five or six figures for the right total solution.

Let's take it a step further. In the Speak Your Way To Cash® Academy, we had a client land a six-figure contract, and we were able to show her how she could use a percentage of that contract to subcontract the work. That simply means that the contract was large enough that she could hire other speakers and consultants under her to help fulfill the deliverables of the contract. You can't subcontract when the overall value is too small. You will have to do *all* that work yourself. Keep that in mind. When you charge more, you can give other people work opportunities.

When I realized that *multiple* clients were hiring multiple speakers and consultants for services that I could provide, I had to change my attitude. I couldn't sit around and ask why these clients were not asking me to come back. Instead, I needed to tell clients about my ultimate offer *every* time. The moment you make this realization for yourself, you might feel overwhelmed. Should you pitch a $100,000 package every time? Assemble a proposal with multiple products and services? That sounds exhausting only because you don't have a process for assembling and inviting clients to work with you. When I got my first $1,000 check for speaking, I didn't have an organized process either. When I finally created and implemented more structure in my business, I went from four figures to five figures to six figures and beyond. If you want to be able to pitch the CEO of PepsiCo in the airport or transform lives, you need to know how to write a substantive proposal.

Putting a Six-Figure Corporate Offer Together

A lot of my clients have no packages ready when they enter Speak Your Way To Cash®. That's okay! Once you commit to the mindset of landing six-figure corporate speaking contracts, you will want to explore the possibilities and the packages that put that cash in your pocket. Assembling a package isn't just about picking and choosing a few products and services. You need to set up a system in which you are researching the best services for your clients and using data to refine these packages time and time again.

The processes we set up in Speak Your Way To Cash® will follow you from the moment you decide to assemble a package to your first booking. Additionally, it will follow you after the engagement has finished, and you have received feedback. This system starts with market research. My client, Dorianne, joined the Speak Your Way To Cash®

Academy after already having some success as a speaker and consultant. However, she hadn't landed the six-figure corporate speaking contract she was seeking. About halfway through the program, she did it! She landed a six-figure speaking contract, and she did not throw the kitchen sink into the proposal. Instead, she learned about what others were charging, stood firm in the value that she provided, and pitched. She did note in her Speak Your Way To Cash® Podcast episode that she was nervous to send the contract. She waited days to send it. Then, she anxiously waited for them to sign it. They signed, and she did her happy dance and told us about it in the private Speak Your Way To Cash Academy Facebook group! It was a huge win for all of us. I want to see you doing a happy dance so let's discuss market research that will help you develop your large package!

Market Research

Market research is so important. I could write an entire chapter on how to conduct market research and gather information from potential clients. The purpose of market research is to understand the "what" that your clients are seeking in their packages. However, there are smaller goals you should focus on as well. Market research will help you uncover the *language* that your clients are using. How do they describe their problems? How do they explain their solutions? When they have a problem, are they likely to hold a workshop in the office or look for events that their employees can attend on their own time? Market research will help you "talk the talk" as you're assembling packages and pitching to clients. Clients want to know that you understand them. When they feel seen and understood, they are more likely to trust you and invest their money in your services.

Another goal of market research should be to discover what your clients need. What training do HR directors need to handle changes to laws and policies throughout their state properly? What pivots feel most daunting to CEOs in a post-COVID-19 world? Your packages provide solutions, but you won't know how to provide solutions to problems that you cannot identify. In law school, the hardest skill-set for students to grasp is issue-spotting. I wrote the book, *The Law School Hustle*™, to teach law students how to spot issues and grow their legal careers while they are in school! Issue-spotting isn't just hard for students; it's hard for entrepreneurs and corporate professionals too. Listen in. Your main job as a business owner is to spot problems, not to complain about them. You also should be focused on providing solutions. You can't show up demanding top rates if you can't issue-spot! Identify the problem; be the solution; charge for the transformation. That's what you have to do.

I break down the ins and outs of market research in the Speak Your Way To Cash® Academy, but I'll tell you this. LinkedIn is a great source for market research. You can use it to conduct interviews and get feedback on what people with certain titles need from you.

I say "people with certain titles" because you will need to know which persons you're going to contact when you start pitching your packages. Do you want to reach HR directors, COOs, or the directors of student affairs? Each of these different positions has different budgets, problems, and needs they want to discuss. Narrow down the people *you* want to pitch and set up interviews. By the way, a virtual assistant or research assistant can help you with this process.

Market research will help you generate leads, but you don't have to invite people to experience your products and services at the research phase. This phase really is designed to gather information. In fact, when I am asking people to do a market research call with me, I explicitly say that I am not trying to sell them anything, but rather, I am hoping to learn more about their industry for my research. To prepare, put together 5-10 questions about what people are seeking, what their problems are, and what solutions make sense to them. Use this opportunity not only to understand what your clients want in a package but also to build relationships with potential clients, learn their language, and start building a list of leads to invite to work with you down the line.

Putting Together a Long-Term Package

In the Invite section, I share how you can use your knowledge of your client's industry to co-create a vision and assess their long-term goals. This happens during the "discovery call," that call you make before you send over a proposal or sign any contracts. During the discovery call, you will need to put together a long-term package to help your client achieve their goals and lay out the vision you have created together. This package is *not* just going to include a one-time engagement.

What goes in that package? The answer will depend on you, your client, and the information you discuss in the discovery call. However, you should have a handful of events or offerings that you are ready to pull out and assemble into that package before you pick up the phone. Here are just some common products and services that speakers include their packages:

- Workshops

- Keynote speeches

- Multi-day events

- Licensing

- Consulting sessions

- Executive coaching sessions

- Audits on company culture

- Focus groups

- Executive roundtables

- Panels

- Retainers with regular consults and check-ins

- Access to coaching materials

- Surveys and assessments

- Plan design

- Executive or leadership training

Reread the section on selecting your topic because when I discuss monetization, I provide specifics about items you can include in your speaking proposal. Do the items listed above sound like one-time events? No. These packages bring you back to your clients again and again. When clients invest in a six-figure package with workshops, coaching sessions, and access to exclusive materials, they are benefitting from your gifts and knowledge for months at a time. That access is worth the six-figure price tag!

You can look to other speakers or business owners in your industry for inspiration, but the beauty of these packages is that they are *customizable*. Customize your package based on what your clients want and what *you* are comfortable providing. If you don't love hosting or sitting on panels, you don't have to include those things in your package! Are you still building a course of your own? There is no rush. Just add it to your package next quarter or next year. Add the products and services that excite you. When you're excited to show up for your clients, they will get more out of your offer.

Also, nothing is "unlimited". You should make sure that you are clear about the amount of time the client is buying. One huge mistake speakers and entrepreneurs make is thinking that because a client is paying a premium, they have to throw in unlimited calls and a lot of other "stuff" to "live up to" the value of the package. Don't do that. First, deal with your mindset. People want a high-quality product or service. They don't want a whole lot of stuff that may or may not create the transformation they want. Do not offer unlimited calls. Instead, make it clear that "up to 120 minutes of consulting is included."

Do not offer 10 workshops for $50,000 when you want your average workshop price to be $15,000 or more. Make sure your pricing makes sense. For instance, if it's $15,000 for one workshop, my package may include four workshops for $60,000, but they each include a digitized companion that employees can use for years to come. If they purchase the one-off workshop outside of a package, the additional materials are not included. You also could offer a slight discount for bulk booking, but it has to make sense. We will go even deeper into the pricing discussion in the next section!

Add the Price Tag

Before you hold any discovery calls, you should know what you are going to charge for each offer within your package. If you charge $7,500 for a keynote speech and $10,000 to hold a workshop, you can put together a package of two keynotes and six workshops for a nice $75,000. Add in a 60-minute pre-event consultation for $2,500, and you can up your fee even more. (See the previous example just before this section.) If a client tells you that they're only interested in four workshops and the pre-event consultation, you both know that the package is going to be $42,500. You could decide that what you presented them was bulk pricing, so you can do a portion of the package, but it may cost a bit more because they aren't getting the bulk pricing. This is called positioning.

The way you present your price is crucial. Above all else, it needs to be clear and give them certainty that you aren't just making this up out of thin air. From start to finish, the buying process should give your client confidence in you. If you are fumbling over numbers or are uncertain about what you are charging, that confidence is lost. People pay to follow leaders; they won't pay to follow you if you seem directionless. You have to lead them confidently through the sales process. When you are selling your expertise, your client has to start following you from the very first interaction. You must start leading from the onset. Remember, you are leading and guiding your clients through the sales process in the same manner that you will guide them during your time as their consultant or trainer. Be confident. Be clear.

Some speakers charge their clients by the hour instead of by the event. I don't. Why? The money that goes into every event doesn't always come with an hourly fee. I teach value-based pricing, and I budget everything that provides value to my services into that price. How do you prepare for your services? Do you sit down and write a speech? Do you practice it? Do you get graphics created? Do you hire an instructional designer to make sure it suits diverse learning styles? Do you work with a comedian to ensure you use humor correctly and impactfully? Are you traveling?

I don't just budget my time. I have a whole team of people help-ing me prepare. Before each speech, I pay an instructional designer to help me organize my materials for diverse learning styles; I budget the instructional designer's rate into my rate. I pay a graphic designer to make flyers for the event, and I budget that cost into my rate. I pay my virtual assistants to send out emails and schedule calls before and after an event. Everyone that I pay to help me elevate my speeches cost money. That goes into my rate! The most important thing that impacts my pricing is the value of the transformation I will help that company or college achieve. It's priceless, but we find a way to put a price on it. To be clear, the price we give still allows them to get a significant return on their investment.

When you consider how much time, money, and effort goes into a single speaking engagement, you'll see why $500 just isn't enough. The average professional speaker charges $7,500 for a single keynote speech. The number that works best for *you* depends on your budget and the amount you want to make as a professional speaker. If you are comfortable doing 20 engagements a year to make $100,000, you can charge $5,000 for a single keynote speech and hit your financial goals. However, if you're looking to make $250,000 and only work with 10 clients a year, it's time to raise your rates and pitch packages that hit at least $25,000.

Have Pricey Opt-ins Ready

Before you pick up the phone, you should be able to say your price confidently. You may need to practice saying it in the mirror. The first time you say your speaking fee should not be on the phone with the client. I mean, you can do that, but oftentimes, it sounds more confident if you've practiced it first. How much is a single workshop? How much is a one-year license to view your signature speech? How much is an assessment of company culture? You should also have an opt-in that clients can use to "try out" your products and services.

Not every client is going to say yes to a $75,000 package right away. They might have to consult with their budget or consider you for next year. That's okay. I always have an opt-in or downsell ready to go to offer if the client passes on the larger package. After hearing you present a $75,000 package, the $12,500 keynote speech feels much more affordable. They accept that rate, and you can hang up the phone happily! That is what I call a pricey opt-in. They try out one service one time, and you crush it. Then, you revisit the full proposal on the post-event wrap-up call! This is just the call you have after the event to make sure you exceeded your client's expectations!

Having this opt-in offer ready will leave the door open to continue your relationship with your client and pitch that $75,000 package again. Once your client has experienced what you have to offer for $12,500, they'll understand the value you provide and see the skills you have to provide a long-term transformation for their organization. That $75,000 will be easier to spend because the client already likes you. They wouldn't have this opportunity to see you at work if you didn't have this opt-in ready to offer on your discovery call. As a general rule, clients love spending money with outside companies they like!

Let Clients Build Your Package For You (Discovery Call)

I can't give you the perfect package because I don't know your specific clients or industry. I also don't know how often you want to travel, how often you want to speak, or what your personal preference is for certain events. Market research will direct you toward the best products and services for your clients. Your *clients* will confirm whether these choices sell. Let your clients work with you to co-create a vision and assemble the right services. As you get to know your industry and your clients, you'll learn what works, what doesn't work, and what resonates with your audience. In the Speak Your Way To Cash® Academy, I give feedback on my students' corporate speaking proposals. What I will do in chapter nine is give you some elements to include in your proposal, so you have a good outline to get started. (This will suffice until we work together one-on-one or in my program!)

In later chapters, I'll share how I use data and feedback to transform the packages I offer and pitch to new clients. A quick Google Form will tell you everything you need to know about the demand for the different products you can offer. Don't worry about creating the perfect package right now. The more engagements you book, the more obvious your ultimate offer will be. Figure out what works for you and your goals.

Selling is all about chasing the "no." However, let's think about the "yes" for a minute. After weeks and weeks of pitching to clients, that "yes" is going to feel sweet. How sweet? The answer depends on your package. When your client says "yes" to a $50,000 package, you're going to feel like every "no" was worth the effort, but if you don't price correctly or only pitch one-time engagements, those wins are not going to feel as sweet.

Meet Kevin Goins

If you made it this far, you see yourself as a six-figure speaker. Do you want to bring in seven figures every year? Since you kept reading, I'm going to drop some truth. Do you want the truth about six-figure and seven-figure speakers? Here it is. Six-figure speakers may not have products in their offers, but seven-figure speakers *definitely* have products. Seven-figure speakers either have backend products that they promote during their speeches, or they have products available *in addition* to their speeches.

I dropped this gem on Episode 77 of my podcast: *How To Engage In B2C High-Ticket Sales As A Speaker With Kevin Goins*. If you want a masterclass in sales, you have to listen to this episode. Kevin is a speaker who runs the Client Building Academy. He started his career as a pharmacist, but always knew he was a speaker. Kevin eventually found the confidence to go down this path after attending events held by speakers, including my Speak Your Way To Cash® Live event. He found so much value in the live event that Kevin booked a VIP Day with me.

When Kevin was ready to pursue speaking heavily, he put together a tour to different pharmacy schools. There were no big packages and no retainers. It was just a tour of different engagements. COVID-19 had other plans. The tour was canceled. Fortunately, people saw Kevin's talent and sales acumen. They started outsourcing sales to him. He was putting people in high-ticket courses, and when I say high-ticket courses, I mean $3,000 and up.

This gave Kevin an idea. He had a skill that people needed. He thought, *Why not sell that? Why not put together an entire academy to show people how they can invest in themselves?* That's what he did. He built the Client Building Academy, a product in which he can share *his* skills with salespeople and business owners.

Another gem that I dropped during this episode is the idea of "investment before transformation." Kevin was invested in a VIP Day with me before he made his big transformation as a speaker and business owner. Booking a VIP Day isn't cheap! With the knowledge he gained from the VIP Day, he was able to invest in *himself* and set up his business. Kevin's clients are making an investment with him before they are transformed into salesmen who can enroll high-ticket clients and transform *their* careers. Your clients will do the same when they invest in *your* five to six-figure packages and products.

Kevin has attended workshops, courses, and other events held by speakers. He's dropped $7,000 or $10,000 because he knows the value he gets from high-end speaking events. That's why his products and packages aren't cheap! No one is going to believe that a $500 course is going to change lives. They're paying for information that will transform their lives forever! That's worth way more than $500.

When you put together a package, you have to keep this in mind. Other people will buy what you're selling. If you're feeling uncomfortable charging high-ticket prices, analyze this. Is it because you don't invest heavily in yourself? Is it because you have some money mindset issues you need to address? Are you teaching a topic in which you still need some experience? Analyze it and deal with it because there's always a reason! When you believe that your gifts have the potential to transform lives, your clients will too. They will be *excited* to spend money. They will *want* to shell out $3,000, $5,000, $10,000, or much more to spend time with you. Once you know how to communicate your gifts, you can do that in any number of ways. Remember, they won't buy until you believe, and you won't take the actions to get them to buy until you believe!

I attract true experts, and speakers like Kevin Goins are true experts. The gems we dropped in his podcast episode are just a taste of what "investment before transformation" truly means. You picked up this book because you are a true expert, and you have a gift that is worth more than money can buy. The services you offer in your six-figure proposal should reflect this truth.

We've covered a lot of information in this chapter. If you don't remember anything else, remember:

- You have to conduct market research to hear how your client explains their problems and solutions.

- Select the solution you give the client based on the client's needs and your desire to provide the service. Don't sell a service you don't want to provide.

- Never offer a one-time speech to a client. Instead, offer the ultimate solution every time.

- If a client isn't prepared to invest in the ultimate solution, be sure to give them a "pricey opt-in," so they can get a feel for your services. Remember, this one-time service is only offered if they aren't ready to move forward with the ultimate solution.

Act Your Way to Cash™

Get out your notebook and make a list of every expense that goes into one keynote speech. How much time or money would you ideally spend putting together a PowerPoint presentation? Do you spend time in your car driving to events? Do you pay for your hair, nails, or a fresh fit for each engagement? Don't be shy with these expenses. These expenses are just the reality of being a speaker who brings value to their clients. If you don't have a team, assign a rate to each hour that you spend preparing for an engagement. Add up all of these expenses. These are your expenses as a speaker. If you accept anything less than this, you are in the negative!

Now you've got your expenses. If you charge any less than this number, you are paying to speak and losing money in the process. That's an important number to have. Did you know that the average full-time professional speaker charges $7,500? Are you an average speaker? Do you provide an extraordinary result? Choose your number for a one-time talk. Use this number to start setting rates for everything in your packages. This number should be what I call your "get out of bed" number. I am not getting out of my bed for an engagement less than _____. Fill that number in for yourself here! Write it out!

_____

_____

_____

_____

_____

Chapter 9

Assembling Your Six-Figure Proposal

My signature speech is called "The Currency of Confidence®." Even though this is my signature speech, I typically don't pitch it as just a keynote speech. When I pitch The Currency of Confidence® program, I often pitch it as a three-part workshop series and an assessment. Why? Although a keynote will help, you can't build confidence overnight, which means I need to work with clients over time to get them the transformation they want.

Give Them More Opportunities To Hire You

Your proposal should present your client with the grandest picture of what you can provide over the course of a month, a quarter, or a year. They can choose to purchase only a portion of the proposal, but at least they know how you can serve them. When I first started out, I'd sell only keynotes and workshops, so clients would be shocked to learn that I could coach their leaders, convert the workshop into a series, and provide an assessment for them. Now, they don't have to wonder. They know I can provide a variety of solutions that are all based on the same proprietary framework.

Elements of a Great Proposal

If this is your first time putting together a proposal, don't worry. I got you. I'm dropping all the quick tips and gems you need to put together a professional proposal that you can send over to clients after your initial call. A great proposal contains six different elements:

- Personal Introduction
- Executive Summary
- Initial Proposed Engagement
- Details and Pricing
- Terms and Conditions
- Closing

Personal Introduction

Who are you? What is your story? Start off your proposal with a brief introduction. Remember those short and long bios that you put together for the press? They come in handy when you're putting together your proposal and pitching to clients. However, this particular biography should not just be your biography, but it should weave in your company's brand story. It should answer the question of why you do this work.

Executive Summary

What does your client need? Executive summaries should offer a brief explanation of the vision that you have created with your client and the ways your solutions can make that vision come to life. Don't go into too many details here. Just focus on objectives. For example, "Based on our call, it is clear to me that COMPANY X has three key objectives…"

Initial Proposed Engagement

Where are you going to start? The initial proposed engagement section should provide an overview of the services your client should purchase. Explain why these services will provide solutions to the problems that your client is facing. For example, "We suggest COMPANY X start with the following to achieve its objectives: (a) 3 Executive Roundtables, (b) 3 All Staff Trainings, and (c) Up to 10 hours of Executive Coaching. This engagement will cost $_____."

Engagement Details and Pricing

When your clients get a proposal, I guarantee this is the section they are most interested in seeing laid out. It's the section with the dollar sign on it! This is the section where you can show your clients everything you will do for them *and* the cost for each service. Clearly explain your offer and discuss what this specific package includes. Don't forget to write how long the engagement will last. Your clients may want extra services, longer calls, or add-ons. Make it clear that your package does not include extra "a la carte" items. They have to pay for sides. Also, be sure to detail what goes into the items listed. Don't simply list "Workshop." Rather, use more descriptive wording such as, "Workshop, including the instructional design of one workshop with up to 45 minutes of customized content, a 15-minute Q&A, a digital companion guide, and a pre-event survey to assess the audience's needs." That may sound like a lot, but a digital companion guide can be a one-page fillable PDF, and a pre-event survey can be a 5-question Google form that they send to their employees beforehand because it will help you tailor your speech to the audience. Remember, your speech and your proposal should focus on your framework. Everything you do should follow your framework. That's what makes you unique!

Clear Next Steps (Terms and Conditions)

This is a brief section where you include information about how you get paid for the engagement and how clients can access additional services. Keep this simple. Do you require a deposit upfront? Can the client pay in installments? Is there someone on your team who the client can contact for questions? As you start to work with clients who accept your proposal, you'll learn what you want to add to this section. It should address questions that typically come up after you send the proposal.

Closing

Wrap it up! I like to add a simple overview to my proposals. I include brief information about my framework and contact information to schedule an appointment. Don't stress too much about this section. It can be two to three sentences.

Quick Tips for Assembling a Great Proposal

Now that you have everything that you need, it's time to refine your proposal. This document is going to be asking for six figures! You need it to be clear and professional.

Remember your brand colors, fonts, etc.

The fully designed proposal should incorporate your brand colors and fonts. If you don't have brand colors get on it. When your color scheme is established, you can make an on-brand proposal yourself and have a graphic designer make it pretty for you!

Work with a copywriter

Here's a little secret about me. I don't love writing proposals. I write the first cut of the proposal just to make sure it has all the information needed, and then, I usually work with a copywriter who can make it sound amazing. We have someone in-house who is great, and here's a secret. Chris (my husband) is an amazing writer too. If you have a copywriter on your team, you can send bullet points to that person. Give your team members the task of developing strong, clear language that communicates your professionalism.

Put your proposal in a PDF and Word document

If you do outsource this task to a copywriter, ask the copywriter to make the file a PDF *and* a Word document. Having a Word document on hand makes it easy if you need to make quick changes for different clients. PDFs look pretty. Keep both files in the same folder for easy access. Tailoring each proposal to your client shouldn't require more than a few quick fixes that you can go in and review before hitting "send." This is an important point; you should not be writing full-on proposals for small engagements of $15,000 or less. That simply requires a clear contract and often an email. If you are writing a proposal, you should have a standard proposal that you can edit quickly for each client. Remember, you are selling your framework that's the same. It undergirds all your trainings, consulting sessions, and similar resources. You simply are repackaging that single framework in a number of different ways that you enjoy. You should not be starting from zero to write a brand new proposal each time. Clients buy what you sell so sell them services you enjoy providing that will help them. You can do some tailoring of your proposals per client, but you should not be writing a new proposal from scratch for each client. If you do, you will be doing work you are not paid to do. Work smart, not necessarily hard.

Here are some key things to remember from this chapter:

- Your proposal should be clear, error free, and on-brand. Ideally, it should display your brand story at the beginning.

- You should include services that you enjoy and detail what's included in each service they are getting.

- Nothing in your proposal should be unlimited. Be sure to detail clearly what time parameters apply to your services.

- Make your proposal on-brand. It should look nice.

Act Your Way to Cash™

This one is easy. Write a six-figure proposal! Even if you don't have the language down, write some bullet points and put together a sample package that you anticipate offering your clients. You need to see how your proposal will look and what content you want to include. You can even make it pretty by hopping on Canva and taking an hour to put together a mock proposal that you might send to clients who are interested in your services. Then, post the cover page to your six-figure proposal in the Speak Your Way To Cash® Facebook Group!

Part Four

Invite

Chapter 10

Setting Up the System
To Get You Leads

The reason speakers have an issue with selling is that they believe that they are asking someone to do them a favor. In reality, when you sell your services, you are serving them. I had a client tell me that she wasn't going to join the Speak Your Way To Cash® Academy, but because I followed up with her and told her she should 100% join based on her goals, she did! Six months into the program, she thanked me for inviting her to the program. She said she knew she needed to join but needed to be pushed. Similarly, I had a large pharmaceutical company that I pitched to bring me in to do some training. Afterwards, I told them more ways we could keep working together. They were so grateful. People love being invited to work with you. They don't want to be pushed, but who doesn't want an invitation to something good? You are the something good. Your services are excellent. Invite them to work with you! Let's talk about pitching. When I say "pitch," I really mean "invite." Pitching a product sounds like you're convincing people to do something they're not interested in doing. However, *inviting* people to have an experience is much more appealing.

Are you more likely to say "yes" if someone is pitching you the idea of going to a $2,000 conference or if someone is inviting you to network with professionals who will elevate your career? The second option is more appealing because you know what you're getting out of the event. Every pitch should be an invitation *and* a gift. You are giving potential clients the opportunity to make their visions a reality through your services.

I see speakers forget this all the time. They feel that pitching is more like begging than gifting. These speakers are giving up their power seats before they even sit down. The products and services you are offering to your clients are mutually beneficial. You get paid, and your clients are transformed for life. Potential clients who turn you down miss out on an investment in themselves, their employees, or their students. Don't take it personally. Walk away and have a plan for following up when the person is in a better position to invest. If someone didn't accept a gift from you, you might be a little confused, but it shouldn't ruin your day! While you may want to work on the positioning of your services, it shouldn't stop you from inviting people to work with you. That applies here. You will be told "no" a lot! People who get a lot of yesses typically get ten or twenty times as many nos. If you don't have the success you want, you likely just haven't failed enough to get it.

When I left my multi-six-figure job, I gave speeches based on my book, *The Law School Hustle*™. All of my speeches took place at law schools, and my goal was to promote and sell my book. I wasn't speaking my way to cash at that point. To make money, I was focused on selling books. If a law school didn't pay me to stand up in front of their students and speak, I had to hope that I would sell enough books to pay the bills.

To set up a speaking tour, I pitched 300 colleges a week. You read that right—a week. I probably pitched 4,000 clients total to set up my tour and promote *The Law School Hustle*™. You want to know how many clients I landed during that time?—25. I landed 25 out of the 4,000 clients I pitched, and I didn't have a system like I have now. Sending out 300 pitches a week was as exhausting as it sounds *because* I didn't leverage every yes into a larger package. I sold books and a keynote. That was it.

I want you to be pitching every week when you put down this book. The *only* way you can do that without spending all of your time and energy on pitches is to set up a CRM (a customer relationship management tool) that manages all of your invitations and leads. Don't sleep on the information I'm about to share with you! Trust me; it will make invitations *so much easier.* No one wants to copy and paste 300 random emails into Gmail each week. You have to use a good CRM with automations. Front loading *today* will put more cash in your pocket tomorrow (And I'm talking about a metaphorical "tomorrow" because closing deals takes time).

Step It Up and Set Up Your System

Invest in a CRM

First, I have to ask you, "Do you have a CRM?" If you don't have one, get one. A CRM helps you manage all of the communications you have with your clients and leads. I don't know about you, but my email is stuffed every single day. Don't let leads drop out of your funnel because your inbox is a mess. Let the CRM handle everything.

If you've never used a CRM before, you're not alone. Do you remember Brittany Sherrell? She had never used a CRM before working with me. She didn't understand the power of using a CRM to pitch and organize her contacts. Now, she says that one of the most crucial systems in her larger strategy is that CRM. CRMs don't just give you a broader reach of contacts. You can connect with them on a deeper level. All of your notes from a call? They're in the CRM. Do you have reminders created to follow up with each contact? A CRM does that. Introducing Brittany to a CRM gave her the chance to reach the masses without removing the personal element of emailing each person individually. You can do the same thing.

Invest time and money into your CRM. You can access a CRM for free, but you need to learn *how to use it*. This takes time, and some CRMs are more intuitive than others. There are so many options, and not all plans will be appropriate for the size of your business and your yearly goals. Give yourself the space to research different CRMs and do a demo before you invest in a subscription.

As you grow your business and start to add more contacts to the CRM, you might find yourself paying each month. Make this investment worth your while by thoroughly understanding (and constantly using) the CRM to keep track of contacts. You will find that contacting the press *and* potential clients becomes so much easier with the help of a CRM.

Identify Your Targets

Are you pitching to corporate clients or colleges? Pick one to start and identify your targets. You probably already have some connections based on the market research you've been doing. Build that list. Don't stop once you've started a conversation with one or two people in the position you want to reach. Find new contacts every single day and add them to your list of leads.

At some point, you might want to reach out to a freelancer who can generate these lists for you. I've hired freelancers who generated a list of 1,000 emails and names within 24 hours. That's worth the fee. A freelancer also may be able to help you manage your CRM when it comes time to send out pitches. If you're not outsourcing this process to someone else, LinkedIn is going to be your best friend. Just keep adding to your list and keep track of your progress along the way. One-to-one connections are great! Email people one-to-one but do not spam them and never add them to any lists without their permission.

Do The Research

Having a name and an email are two columns on a much larger spreadsheet. The clients you're inviting probably will receive multiple emails a day from strangers trying to pitch them something. Remember, you're not pitching. You're inviting them to experience your gifts. You have to approach them in a way that you would approach anyone with a gift. Do that by doing your research on each potential client before you start the conversation.

When I first contact a cold lead, I make sure to include personal information. Gather that information when you're identifying your targets and generating lists of leads. Look for people who went to your college, grew up in your hometown, or root for the same football team. (Hey, it works!) I keep notes in my spreadsheets with this information. If you have mutual connections through LinkedIn or other social media networks, be sure to include this information.

Don't Worry About Perfection

Systems always can be changed and refined. Do not worry about having the perfect email or the longest list when you start pitching. You're making big moves in your career right now. Start pitching as soon as you can. Start getting *feedback* from potential clients as soon as you can. No one has the perfect pitch. At our best, my team's email campaign has a 50% response rate. On average, cold emails and other touchpoints have as low as a 3% response rate.

What's the worst a potential client can say? No? That's not so bad. You'll be okay. Once you land your first large contract, you'll see that every potential client who said "no" is just part of your journey to the "yes."

Don't Forget Your Mindset

I'm not sending out 300 pitches a week to land 25 engagements with limited budgets these days. I have a system that allows me to invite clients to work with me for a higher price point now. In the next section, I will go over some strategies that I use. This process required more than just a change to my proposals and systems. I needed to change my mindset too.

In the beginning of my speaking career, I tried to sell my skills and convince people to let me talk on their stages. I don't do that anymore. I realized that people who hire me to speak aren't just buying 45 minutes of me talking on stage. They are *investing* in themselves. They're investing in their students and their employees. I don't want to waste their time, and I don't want them to waste my time. Clients who don't see your services as an investment will be a waste of time. The system for inviting clients to work with you should be set up to avoid wasting anyone's time.

You could be spending time working with clients who are willing to invest $10,000 for one speech or $100,000 for a larger partnership that lasts throughout the year. Therefore, I identify whether clients have a budget before I get on the phone through my discovery call questionnaire. They have to select their budget and identify whether they are ready to book now or in the future. When they note they don't have a budget, I simply have an automated email politely giving them a free resource but asking them to circle back at a better time when they can invest. Obviously, there's a nice way to say this, and I do that, but you get the gist.

Don't get it twisted. People with big budgets will see your services as an investment. C-level executives will see your services as an investment. Even if you haven't sat in the C-suite yourself, you have experiences and gifts that people can use to achieve their goals. When Brittany Sherrell first started pitching, she was intimidated by reaching out to big corporations or people with executive titles. She was coming from a special education background. She didn't have a doctorate or years behind her in research, but that didn't matter. When you work in special education, you have a certain set of skills that other people find valuable. She had all the qualifications she needed to reach out to potential clients and invite them to experience her gifts. The individuals on the other side of her calls and emails are just people. Fancy titles aside, the people to whom Brittany pitches, the people to whom you pitch, and the people to whom I pitch are just people. The questions are, "Which people are the right people? Which people see the value of your gifts? Which people have the budget and the authority to sign a contract and hand over the cash for you to share your gifts?" These are the questions that need to shape your invitation strategies.

Before I had a system in place to identify my targets and do proper research, I didn't care who was on the other end of my emails. I didn't care who was on the phone. I didn't care if the people booking me saw my speech as an investment or saw me as just a speaker to fill the time and use up their student activities budget. All I cared about was whether they were going to say "yes" to my pitch. Did they want me on stage? Did they have at least some money in their budget? Then, I wanted to work with them.

Now, my mindset is different. I don't work with people with whom I don't want to work. My pre-consult questionnaire filters out clients who may be difficult or who just don't fit my brand. My time is too precious, and my rate is too premium to be spent on people who I'm not excited about helping. If it's not the right fit for me, I want every potential client to find the best speaker/consultant for them. That's not always me, and that's okay! I refer out a lot of work! I'm not getting out of that power seat anytime soon! That's what you have to remember when you're setting up your CRM and inviting people to work with you. Do you want to work with them or are you just giving them a call because you want to close the sale? If you choose the second, drop the phone and find the next potential client in your CRM.

Stop Applying to Speak

The P.A.I.D. Method™ and the system I use to invite clients to book with me might look a lot different than the one you're using now to book speaking engagements. In the past, you may have applied to speak at conferences or landed a one-time engagement with a client who didn't want to *invest* in the gifts that you have to share. I've been there too. These are small wins. Small wins are great every now and again, but Speak Your Way To Cash® isn't about stopping at the small wins. We want big wins too. We want $25,000 wins, $100,000 wins, and $500,000 wins. Working for a $1,000 win every day quickly became exhausting for me. One or two $500,000 wins a year is *exhilarating*. You won't get there by filling out a quick application with 1,000 other speakers. You need a system that moves *paying* clients through your sales funnel. Building your sales plan is going to take longer than it does to send your speaking reel to a conference. That's okay. Think of the big wins. Think of the ways that five to six-figure contracts will support you as you continue moving through this book.

Keep in mind that your big wins often force you to *walk away* from small money while you build systems and develop a six-figure offer. Big wins don't come overnight. Setting up your proposal will take time. Your first packages won't be perfect. Your response rate may be around 3%, and the rate of clients who book you will be much lower. Do not quit. Do not take it personally if a client doesn't respond to your email or if a potential client doesn't schedule a call after attending your webinar. Everyone is not going to make it through your entire process. The ones who do are going to be ready to invest. Remember that.

How Do You Reach Out to Leads?

The next two sections will break down the ways that you reach out to leads and invite them to become clients. You do not have to use both methods, but you *can* use both methods successfully. Cold calling isn't dead. Even if you don't have an inside sales background, you can pick up the phone and send out an email to nurture and convert leads. I personally *prefer* to host events. Both of these options are available to you, pandemic or no pandemic. Explore both options *and* try them out as you set up your system and Speak Your Way To Cash®.

Direct Selling

Direct selling is just that—sending an email or picking up the phone to reach a potential client. Maybe this is someone you saw on LinkedIn. Maybe it's not. If you have done your research and found people who are in a position to hire you and have a *budget* to hire you, your invitation should feel like a gift. This is why I'm stressing the importance of conducting market research and digging more deeply to find a personal connection between you and your leads. Don't waste too much time pitching to someone who doesn't have the authority to invest in bringing you to their workplace. Initially, you will have to spend some time finding out who the right people are. How do you do this? Well, if you aren't working with me as your personal speaking coach, you will need to find the job titles and pitch a fair amount of people with that title. When you see who responds and who is interested, you will have to look for trends. What's the company size of those who responded? Where are they located? What month did you get the most traction? From those trends, you will focus more on the people who say yes and companies like them and less on the companies that say no. You also can get referrals from past clients!

Sending an email is less intimidating than picking up the phone, but both of these options could work for you. Don't worry about perfection. The right touchpoints will become clear to you as you start inviting people to work with you. LinkedIn messages and personalized cards in the mail are some of the ways to reach your contacts and start the conversation. You won't know what works for you until you take action.

Hosting Events

A critical piece of The Invite Method™ is hosting events. We have an entire module in the Speak Your Way To Cash® Academy focused on how to attract corporate clients with events. Here's the gist. You should host a free webinar that gives an overview of your framework and shares some client success stories. This should be titled something that will intrigue your ideal audience. For example, you could title it "How To Motivate Your Employees Even When They Have Zoom Fatigue Using The AIM Method!" Then, put up an event landing page. If you are techy, you can use a system like Kartra to build your landing page and set up automatic emails to go out before and after the event. However, you can do this in a low tech way and use Eventbrite simply to set up your event—no landing page required. When they register, ask them questions.

You want to know their name, phone number, email, and whether they are interested in resources that will help their employees be more engaged. For the people who say they are interested in that, you know you want to follow up with them. You also could ask them what's their biggest struggle right now with motivating employees! These questions are critical to this strategy. Then, you want to invite people to the event. I do this via LinkedIn messages, so you can do that too! In a connection message, just introduce yourself and say, "There's an event coming up that might be of interest to you. My company is hosting_____, and it's complimentary with this invite link [Insert Link]. I thought I would share this information with you!"

I have met some of my best corporate clients by hosting events like this, and they can be short and to the point—45 minutes or less! Less can be more! Again, you are sharing your framework and some quick tips that they can use to improve their workplace but be sure to include client success stories!

Events can help you bring in potential clients who already believe that you have valuable information or skills. You don't have to give away *everything* for free, but you can use these events as an opportunity to introduce yourself, drop some gems, and collect contact information that you can use later when you pick up the phone to pitch.

Here are some key things to remember from this chapter:

- You need a CRM.
- You can either host complementary events, directly message potential customers via LinkedIn, or send them a cold email campaign to invite them to work with you. The method you choose is up to you.
- Focus on the big wins and avoid activities that may lead to results that feel good but are not in alignment with your goals. In summation, avoid applying to speak. Take clients through your sales process.
- Remember, there are clients who will be thrilled to work with you, but you have to find them and invite them to work with you.

Act Your Way to Cash™

Get yourself a CRM! This is crucial to automating your sales process. A CRM is also much easier to hand off to a virtual assistant or team member. Spend an hour or two playing around with your CRM, adding leads, and maybe sending out an email or two. Once you've selected a CRM, shoot me an email to ashley@speakyourwaytocash.com with the subject line "CRM." Let me know which one you are using! Here is a pro tip. Make sure the CRM has email sequences—the ability to send a series of emails automatically based on the actions a person takes when they receive the email!

Chapter 11

Handling Sales Calls With Ease

Conversations close deals. Conversations convert. Conversation closed. You absolutely need to get great at verbalizing how you will help clients! As a recap, here is a typical sales process. You send an email inviting clients to work with you. In that email, you ask them to book a call with you. They book a call expressing their interest. When they book that call with you, the call should last for no more than 30 minutes. In the form they use to book the call, you ask them all the formalities including the budget, the event date, the key pain point that led them to book the call, and maybe another creative question that will help you analyze how you can serve them. Then, you get on the call. What happens next? You have to lead the call. Start sitting in the seat of the expert from the first call. You will set the stage for the call, and you will guide the call, but they should be doing the vast majority of the talking. In this section of the book, we are going to go over what you need to know to have productive sales calls that close deals!

When you are having a conversation with a potential client re-member you need to want to work with them too. When I talk to a lead for the first time, I use the call as a way to learn whether they will be a good fit for me as well. This way, when the contract is signed, and the money is in my pocket, I'm excited to share my gifts. Those who want nothing always have everything. You have to remove every ounce of desperation from your body before you pick up that phone. If you don't get that person as a client, it's okay. It's likely for your good. You don't want to lose a client because you're unprepared, but you are des-perate for nothing. The best mindset shift I made in my life was this; *nothing happens to me. Everything happens for me—no matter what.*

Remember the Person on the Other End of the Line

After clients have booked a call with you, they are warm to you. At a minimum, they know who you are, and they have agreed to pay you in time. Don't take that vote of confidence for granted. Time is often more valuable than money because it can't be replaced. I tell my clients all the time that we pitch *to people, not platforms.* Start your calls with prospective clients by thanking them for their time and letting them know exactly what you want to cover during the call. Then, ask them whether they had anything they wanted to discuss in addition to what you plan to cover during the call.

Ask Fact-Finding Questions

We give a sales script to everyone in the Speak Your Way To Cash® program. It outlines the bare bones of how your conversion conversation should look. The script starts with a roadmap to introducing yourself and explaining the purpose of the call (see above). You make a connection with the client, say who you are, and make it clear that you are going to guide the conversation in a way that does not waste time. Remember, this call is about ensuring that you want to work with the client too. Once you introduce yourself, you're going to start fact-finding.

When I say fact-finding, I mean asking questions. The goal of this process is to "create a vision" with the client. That's no easy task. These questions get deep. What is the vision that your client wants? How does your client measure success? What is holding the client back from achieving this vision at their company or college? How has their organization changed since they first started at the company? By listening to these answers, you can co-create a vision for them that includes the products and services that you offer.

By doing this, you discuss the possibility of forming a partnership. You're not just trying to "get away" with selling them a six-figure package. I know that getting on the phone with a potential client makes a lot of people feel icky. They don't want to push something on clients, and they don't want to appear desperate while doing it. You can't properly sell a product or service to someone if you're desperate. The client will sense it right away. People usually can tell when you want something from them. We're chasing the "no," remember? Chasing the "no" is about wanting nothing. If you approach a sale because you *need* to close the deal, you've walked away from your power seat.

Fact-finding and conversion conversations should be about seeing whether *you* can deliver the vision that your clients want for their businesses. Sometimes, you are going to realize that you can't deliver that vision. The client might not have the budget. The client may want too much of your time, or the client may have problems that you can't solve. That's okay. The client is more likely to respect you walking away than desperately pitching the wrong solution. You need to pitch the right solution, and it needs to align with how you want to serve your clients. Do you hate consulting? Don't offer it. Do you love workshops? Pitch more workshops in your packages. Do you prefer only working with executives? Pitch executive roundtables. Whatever the solution, make sure you are explaining to them the value of what you have to offer!

Get Permission…

In addition to fact-finding, you will be asking questions in a way that asks for *permission to move forward.* This starts at the very beginning when you explain who you are and why you're calling. "Hey Ms. X, I'm calling today to get a better understanding of your role in your organization and how you envision the organization positively changing for the future. Then, I'm going to talk to you about some of the ways that we've helped clients in the past that are similarly situated to you. Does that sound good?"

If they say "yes," you have permission to move forward. Continue this pattern as you gather facts and learn about the organization. You want them saying "yes" five to seven times before you ever make an offer. This habit does two things. It ensures that you and the potential client are on the same page about where the call is going. Secondly, it helps you listen and focus. One of the things that I teach corporate clients is the L.O.V.E. Method™ of communication. What is the "L" in L.O.V.E? It stands for Listening. Show people you are listening to them by using their language, telling them what they just told you in your own words, and asking for permission to move forward. Check in after gathering facts: "Hey, Ms. X, I'm hearing that what you really want is X, Y, and Z. Am I getting that right?"

Before you make your pitch, you want to get permission one more time. Make sure you are on the same page. "Alright, Ms. X, if I could present a program to you that would improve communication, give your team leads the tools to have difficult coaching conversations, and help improve your overall productivity rating for your company, would you find value in learning more?" Your version of this question will include the three big areas in which the clients noted they need help. You should be using their words here. If you get a "no," then you might have run into some miscommunication. Go back to fact-finding and ask *more* probing questions about their vision and find out what would bring value to their organization. You can't co-create a vision if you don't know what people believe is valuable. Listen to what people want. Note how they are describing their pain points! What are their pain points? How do they envision the way they communicate with their colleagues and their ideal organization? Keep asking questions until you can uncover a holistic solution that people believe is valuable.

...And Pitch!

Now, you have a handful of "yeses" under your belt and permission to move forward with your offer. This is your opportunity to show that you really were listening. Pair your solution with the language that the person used during the fact-finding session. Make sure that potential clients know that your offer is *exactly* what they want. Present your package and explain the value of each offer.

After you explain what you can do for them, incorporate their language. I noted this previously, but I need to repeat this. Before you ask them to buy, you have to ask one more question. "So, Ms. X, does the offer that I presented sound like it will be valuable to your organization?" Ask this *first*. This is a completely different question than, "Are you ready to buy?" If the person sees your offer as something that is valuable, the cost will be inconsequential. You can negotiate price, but you can't sell the person an offer that's not valuable to them. Remember, you already have narrowed down your leads to people in the position to approve your rates. If the person believes that your offer is valuable, but the cost is the barrier between the person and the solution, they will find a way to make it work, or they will keep you in mind for future opportunities. They are not lying when they say this. I had a client cancel a small contract under $10,000 only to recommit and pay over $20,000 as soon as his new budget was confirmed. Confirm the value of your solution before closing the deal.

The #1 reason people struggle with sales is that they make the price the centerpiece of their entire conversation. Think back to Chapter 1—*most speakers only sell to the degree in which they're comfortable buying.* The cost should be inconsequential to your clients. At the end of the day, your call should be about what the client needs and how your proprietary framework would allow you to help them in a way that no other speaker on the planet can. How can you confidently say that no other speaker can offer the same solution as you? That is easy. You're selling them on your signature framework that undergirds every area of your speech. You know and I know that serving people on a high level comes at a price. If you do a great job, your client will be thankful, and the way you say thank you in America is with a check. Remember that. If your clients see the value in your service, they will pay your rate, and you will deliver for them—big time.

"No" Isn't So Bad

Of course, not every person will say yes. That's the reality of inviting people to experience your gifts. Not everybody is going to show up for the party but don't let that hold you back from picking up the phone and asking people to work with you. Every time you're told no over the phone or through an email, you'll realize that nothing changes. Who cares? When you send someone a six-figure proposal, you're not going to get cursed out over the phone. The person is not gonna throw it back in your face.

I remember sending my biggest proposal ever. The package cost $958,000. It wasn't hand-delivered in a fancy package or anything. I just sent it over email. I remember how shaky my hands were hitting that "send" button. I actually was scared to send that proposal! Guess what? Did the client accept the offer? No, the client didn't, but the client didn't beat me up. The client didn't post the email online and drag me through the mud. My reputation remained intact. The only consequence of sending that proposal was that I developed a new relationship with a potential client.

In fact, the client sent me a response asking for a package that was in the $150,000 range. How could I be mad at that? That interaction, shaky hands and all, taught me that nothing bad is going to happen when you put yourself out there. Don't take this as a 100% guarantee. I am a lawyer after all, but even if a client says something salty, you will survive. You can survive anything a client throws at you, and it will make you more resilient when you send out the next proposal.

That $958,000 proposal was a big deal for me. I was so scared to send it out, but I still sent it. If you take one thing away from this chapter, take that away. You may be scared. You may not have a perfect script, a perfect template, or a perfect coach. Guess what? Neither does anyone else. We're going about our days just fine. We're landing five to six-figure contracts, and we don't have all the answers, either. Nothing too bad will happen. If something bad does happen, you can handle it.

Keep Cold Leads Interested

Whether the person on the other end of the line says "yes," "no," or "maybe," leave the person with something valuable. Maybe your client isn't interested in a $150,000 package right now, but the client wants to take you up on doing a one-time speaking engagement. Maybe the client is not interested in hiring you right away at all but wants to listen to your podcast. Keep the client engaged. If the client is a good fit, but just not the best fit right now, follow-up in a quarter.

If you get a "no," don't take it personally. You want to help the client, right? Find a solution that demonstrates your value. Invite the client to take the first steps on a journey to the vision you have co-created. Make sure the client walks away from that call knowing who you are, what you can offer, and where they can find you. Don't wait for the client to find *you*. The final question you should ask is whether the person wants to be added to your mailing list or receive a follow-up call. Set up the next steps before you hang up.

If you feel comfortable, ask for feedback. What could you have done to improve the client's experience on the call? How can you better serve all your clients? If you can walk away from your call with some valuable information about how to improve your client experience, you have "won."

Meet Theresa Harris - Again

Earlier in this book we discussed how Theresa masterfully used her podcast to land a client. Now, we will talk about her resilience in selling to corporations. A "no" isn't so bad, but make sure the potential client *actually says* "no." Pitching to corporate clients sometimes requires that you keep following up *until* you hear "no." Until the person says "no," you're still in the process of pitching to them. No one knows this better than the Scholarship Momma® herself, Theresa Harris.

I have always been truthful with Theresa. When we talked about pitching to corporate clients, I didn't lie to her. I told her that the time between connecting with a corporate client and actually speaking for the client could stretch up to a year's time. That's a long time to secure that check! With that in mind, Theresa was patient when she did find an opportunity to speak with a big corporate client.

Here's what happened. Theresa had coffee with a potential client that was impressed with her services, so she went back to talk to people at her organization and find out who would be the decision-maker to sign Theresa's contract.

The coffee meeting ended, and that next week, Theresa got an email from someone at the organization that could, in fact, hire her. Mind you, this was in early March 2020. The high-school counselor's email told Theresa that although the organization was interested in using her services, they didn't know what was going on. The COVID-19 pandemic had *just* hit, and they didn't know how schooling would look in the next few weeks or months. Instead of trying to book something in March 2020, they asked Theresa to hold off until the fall. That was not a "no." That was an opportunity for Theresa to invite the organization to work with her later in the fall.

Fall came around, and we were still in a pandemic. Schools were still uncertain week to week about whether they would have in-person classes. That didn't matter as much to Theresa, but she didn't hear "no" at any point from the organization. She would still be able to give her speech and provide her gifts to students, teachers, or employees in person or through Zoom. Theresa reached out to the high-school counselor again and asked to be connected to the stakeholders who wanted to hire her. Fortunately for Theresa, I had also hosted a Speak Your Way To Cash® virtual event. In that event, I talked about inviting corporate clients to work with you as a speaker. I included a script for those phone calls with decision-makers. Theresa took that script, made some adjustments to fit her situation, and got on the phone.

Theresa was in with the stakeholders. She was using her script, and she started moving forward with the invitation process. She went back and forth with the stakeholders for a few weeks about the package. At first, they wanted her to do a professional development day. That didn't work out in the contract. Next, they wanted her to speak directly to the students. Instead of just doing one engagement, this organization set Theresa up with six different engagements to talk to six different schools. That was amazing!

The stakeholders scheduled Theresa's six talks for March 2021. Yes, a full *year* after she first connected with the organization, she was able to deliver her speech and share her message with students who wanted to learn more about financial aid. That was a long process, but Theresa was prepared. She successfully reminded the organization that she was still available, even in a pandemic when it was hard to make decisions. She kept herself at the forefront of the organization's mind when it came time to book speakers. Of course, she had the right mindset. Theresa always had the right mindset. After one of my Speak Your Way To Cash® events, Theresa got a box of materials that each speaker receives before the event. In that box are scripts, workbooks, and other materials that help you implement the strategies I'm sharing. Theresa also keeps a reminder in that box. It's a paper that says, "Why not me?" That's the mindset you have to have as you're going through this process. Why not you? Speakers who look like you and have the same amount of experience as you are going out and landing six-figure engagements. Speakers around the world are signing contracts and killing it on stages today. Why not you?

I don't want to wrap up this chapter with Theresa's story just because she's such an inspiring client. Her story provides a powerful example of what it's like to sell to corporate clients and organizations that might come with a lot of red tape. The COVID-19 pandemic certainly created some obstacles during this process, but you might find yourself waiting months before you get booked even after the pandemic. If a corporate client is telling you to reach out in two weeks, two months, or next season, don't worry. That's not a "no." That's an opportunity.

There are processes and systems that your client will need to go through before they sign you. Do not give up hope. You may have to go through a formal bidding process or wait for your contact to get budgetary approval. Do not let this discourage you. Keep following up. Some people follow up with leads every two weeks while they're stuck in limbo. I work faster than that. I pop in every three to five days just to make sure I'm getting one step closer to landing a contract. Follow-up emails don't have to be long, but they have to be sent out. That CRM you've got is really starting to come in handy now, isn't it?

If you're interested in learning more about this topic, take a listen to Episode 83 of my podcast. I talk about the ins and outs of selling to corporations. As you start reaching out to potential leads and doing market research, you might notice that corporations use a different language if they are interested in booking you. They might have a pattern for how they connect you with the decision-makers within their organization. You might find that this year-long wait is just routine in your industry! Use that information as you map out your strategies for today, tomorrow, six months from now, and next year. You might just find yourself signing on the dotted line as Theresa did!

Here's some key takeaways from this chapter:

- Remember that you need to want to work with clients too. It is not just about whether they have the budget to hire you. Sales is a two way street.

- Always follow-up with potential clients and don't lose hope on clients that say "not now" versus "no."

- Make sure you co-create vision with your clients and show that you are listening by repeating back what you heard and having them confirm your understanding.

- Clients should confirm that they find value in your services before you ever ask them to work with you directly.

Act Your Way to Cash™

Call a friend and pitch your services. I'm serious! Have your fact-finding questions in front of you and go through the process of pitching a five to six-figure package. You get bonus points if you have a friend in corporate America, the human resources department, or the director of a department who potentially could hire you! You'd be surprised what your old college buddies are up to now!

Once you invite your friends to learn more about your business, get their feedback. How did you sound on the phone? Could your friend tell that you were listening to their answers? When it came time to share your packages or your rate, did you sound confident? If your friend can't be honest with you, I don't know who can. When you've received some feedback from your friends, head to the Speak Your Way To Cash® Facebook group and let us know how you are going to improve your pitch when you call your next potential client.

Chapter 12

Hosting and Attending Events to Attract Your Ideal Clients

I f you want to speak at colleges, you may already know that there is more than one person who brings speakers to campus. The director of campus programming is the first person to have on your list, but that person is not the only one. Colleges also have student boards that manage their own budgets and have the ability to hire speakers, entertainers, or other people who may attract the student body to events. The director of campus programming often has a hand in managing the student directors of programming, but students may be the ultimate decision-makers. If you didn't know that, now you do.

I open the chapter with this information because hosting events is all about standing in front of the people who potentially could hire you. In 2019, I partnered with the American Professional Campus Association. I did their opening keynote, closing keynote, and a breakout session. That event was dope. Over 50 campuses were present. Directors of campus programming were present along with student boards. Everyone in my ideal audience was right in front of me. I left that event and signed a $5,000 contract with a school. I did one event, and I earned one $5,000 contract. Not bad, but not exactly what I hoped for either. Not to mention, it took several months after the event for me to get that contract signed. There are several campus programming organizations with whom you can partner to speak in front of decision-makers, but you have to pay.

Let me break this down; in my experience, we have generated decent leads from speaking at events where decision-makers are present and ready to hire speakers, but there's a catch. I always got less than my full rate when I did this, so I stopped using this approach. If you are going to hire a speaker at an event where hundreds of other speakers are present, you are likely bargain-shopping. I'm not the bargain speaker. I personally think it still can be beneficial, but just know, they are sometimes looking for a deal at these events. Nonetheless, you can look up a few reputable organizations that have these opportunities such as: NACA—the National Association for Campus Activities, APCA—the Association for the Promotion of Campus Activities, NAMCA—the National Association of Masterminds & Co-Curricular Advancement, and NODA—the Association for Orientation, Transition, and Retention in Higher Education.

Those are organizations that you have to join (there's likely a membership fee), and they will give you a list of others in the organization. Some of them even provide the contact information for their members. In addition to speakers like you, they also have members who hire speakers including college advisors and administrators. They each host national conferences that you can attend and speak in front of folks who may be ideal clients of yours! The only issue is that you will be there with a lot of fellow speakers. That said, it's not a bad way to go; just be aware of what you're up against. Check out Speak Your Way To Cash® Podcast Episode 25 (an older episode, but it discusses a lot of this stuff)!

In addition to speaking at events to get college leads and contracts, I've also spoken at events to gain corporate leads. In this space, I use The Invite Method™ heavily by partnering with organizations to do an exclusive workshop for their audience. In this scenario, I am the only speaker (way better, in my opinion). When I partnered with the Society for Human Resources, I was able to train HR directors from various corporations. During the event, I was allowed to ask the audience members whether they were interested in learning more about my services. A handful of directors raised their hands, and boom, I had a bunch of warm leads to contact. A lot of ideal clients came from that one event. This is a marketing event. You typically are not paid for such an event, but you can be. In the above instance, I was not paid. I looked at it as a marketing expense. Some business owners pay for Facebook Ads to generate leads. Sometimes, as a speaker, depending on the audience, you might pay to speak (rare). When you do, it has to be in front of a well-qualified audience. Let's say you pay $3,000 to speak to 50 of your ideal clients. In the end, you land a $20,000 contract. That's a great return on your investment. Now, it goes south when you're paying to speak or host an event, and you don't close any contracts within six months of the event.

When you are using speaking as a marketing tactic to land paid engagements, here's what you need to have: (1) an incredible talk that gets the audience to like you, shows how you can help them, and displays your framework because that's your unique identifier; (2) an easy way to collect their information (email, phone number, and title); and (3) something to sell them—have your packages and proposals ready to go! Depending on your sales process, you may ask them to book a call if they are interested. Whatever you do, offer something of value, so you can collect their contact information. Here's what I mean. Towards the end of your presentation, you can say, "I've enjoyed speaking with you today. If you would like me to send you an article I wrote detailing some of the tips I've shared here today, text 'KEYWORD' to 777-777-7777!" This should allow you to capture their names and phone numbers.

Here's why I love this! Once you have their phone numbers, you can ask them to give you reviews and schedule a call to learn more about their speaking needs, etc. You want to have a way to contact them and continue your relationship with them! You should get this information before asking them to book a call with you. Remember, when people give you time, they are essentially paying you in a valuable currency that they can't get back. People need a reason to spend time with you—in the professional context anyways!

Where to Find Warm Leads

There are so many opportunities to attend, host, or speak at an event in front of your ideal audience. With the systems that we have described throughout this book, you now have some ideas about where to find leads, and we've even thrown out some job titles you can target depending on your industry. You know the people you want to see in the audience. As you conduct market research, you can ask about events where potential clients will be present. Do you remember way back at the beginning of the book when I said that the number of virtual and in-person events is going to grow every year for the next few years? You have plenty of places to meet your future clients:

- Conferences

- Trade shows

- Meetups
- Association meetings

Think about where your potential clients go to develop professionally. Are you unable to find an event that works for your topic? Host your own! What I teach now is that hosting your own events with decision-makers is the best way to attract quality leads. Make sure the topic is aligned with your framework and invite them to a webinar. It can be a short free webinar on a topic that matters to them. It's an easy way to do market research, generate leads, and get experience explaining your framework. This strategy is the crux of The Invite Method™. Put a webinar together that contains information that is valuable to your clients. Invite everyone who is a cold lead and see who attends or responds to your pitch. Advertise the event on your podcast or on appearances you make in the press. Bring them to you with something that is free or low-cost but still brings some value and shows them who you are. You'll get your chance to warm them up at any event, but an event that you host on your own allows you really to run the show.

Follow Up!

I have been able to get a ton of clients from attending events, but these clients didn't just see me after the event and hand me $20,000. The follow-up is what actually gets you to close on the sale. I got paid $20,000 for my contract back in 2021, a year and a half after I attended the event. You have to be consistent and follow up with the leads who respond to you, express interest in investing in you, and want to work with you. During that process, you can do two things: collect data and build relationships.

Data is crucial to developing your speaking business and providing your clients with the best experience possible. However, following up isn't just about automation and numbers. Send Christmas cards. Send a note of congratulations if the client gets a promotion or if the client's company does really well that year. Before one of my clients signed with me, they reached out to say that they loved the popcorn that I sent them one year for the holidays. Boom. They signed a $60,000 contract a few months later. I'm not saying that the popcorn did it, but the popcorn didn't hurt. Both of these tasks will help you grow your business in different ways. The end goal is to build a business that doesn't burn you out. Data and relationships will get you there.

Follow Up to Collect Data

After I host an event, I send out a survey (often a Google Form) to all attendees. I ask them to fill out the form and give me feedback on the event. Not every attendee fills out the form, but a lot of them do. I take the responses and use them as data to both improve my business *and* get business.

Here's how it works. In the Google Form, I ask the attendees whether they learned something from the presentation. Let's say the attendees are law students, and one of my goals is to land a contract with a law school. I see that 100% of the law students responded that they learned at least one thing from the presentation. 85% of them said they learned more than one thing. The overall rating from the presentation was a 9 out of 10. I bundle all of that information together and use it on my follow-up call with the client.

I also ask about what subjects the attendees want to learn about next. What events would they be willing to attend next? After one event, over 70% of the attendees said they wanted to learn more about mindset. One in three attendees said they would attend a six-week bootcamp just on that subject. This was valuable information that I used when I was building my packages, writing my speeches, and inviting future clients to work with me. I knew what their students wanted. On my follow-up call with the school, I showed them the pie chart that Google Forms generates from the data collected. I showed them that their students wanted additional training on confidence. Having the data to back up your proposed next engagement with a client is very powerful. It makes the "sale" more of a well-researched suggestion to which it is easy for them to agree. Try it out.

Following up and collecting data makes the time you spend at events worth it. I'm not saying you should spend all of your time speaking at events for a low cost because you can gather leads and data. Keep your eyes on the prize and make room for the big contracts. When you take the appropriate action and have a strategy behind speaking to the market and building your clientele, it can be a powerful tool.

Follow Up to Build a Relationship

By now, I have told you a lot about following up: following up with the press, with cold leads, with warm leads, and with potential clients who are just about to sign but have to go through some red tape. Following up is what the business of speaking is all about. Period.

Business is all about relationships. I know a lot of hungry speakers who haven't learned this lesson yet. They host a webinar with 100 leads and don't understand why they weren't able to convert anyone into a client. I ask them how often they followed up with the leads, and I get a blank stare. That's the problem.

Hungry speakers often see their business as the combination of a bunch of transactions. That's not right. Your business is about relationships. Sending out popcorn, following up every five days over email until you hear back, and picking up the phone should all be a part of the way you keep your clients engaged through your sales process. They are seeds that you need to plant, and those seeds are not going to grow overnight. Speaking is not a get-rich-quick scheme. I tell the speakers that I train to start at the top of the speaking market with a six-figure speaking package. That works for them because they are top-quality speakers who can rise up to their six-figure+ price tags. You can do the same.

At the end of the day, you are transforming your clients' lives with your gift. That's no get-rich-quick scheme. That is an honest mission. It's going to take time to fulfill that mission. It will take time to land five to six-figure contracts. Most speakers put in a good 6-12 months of consistent effort before they start seeing real results. Some speakers will land their first contract faster than that, but the sales cycle for corporate contracts can be anywhere from 90 days to six months. It could be longer! During that time, you have to keep following up and building relationships. You have to keep communicating with people. If you put in consistent effort and invite a certain amount of people on the front end, everything will work out.

Here's the other thing. Your goal is not to land any one contract one time. Your goal is to have legacy clients. You want clients to work with you forever. You shouldn't look at people as numbers but as lifelong relationships that will serve your business forever. If the relationship is fruitful on both ends, then you have nothing to worry about. This isn't just about pitching as many people as possible. It's about having a process that consistently narrows the pool of potential clients to the highest value contacts that you should focus on over time. A yes once should be a yes forever if you play your cards right.

Here's what you should take away from this chapter:

- You should plan to host your own event and invite your ideal clients to attend it. This is a marketing event and ensures that you are the only speaker offering a solution to your audience.

- Plan to follow up with potential clients until they tell you "no" definitively.

- You could partner with an organization that already has your ideal audience in attendance, but my favorite approach is to host your own events where you are the only speaker.

- Remember who you are. You are worthy of serving your clients at the highest level and charging for it.

Act Your Way to Cash™

Write down one event that you can host within the next three months. This should be an event that displays your framework. It should be something to which you can invite your ideal clients. Then, I want you to make a landing page for it (or Eventbrite page), connect with decision-makers on LinkedIn, and invite them to attend. Once you see these ideas on paper, you will start to see the possibilities ahead of you.

_____

_____

_____

_____

_____

Part Five

Deliver

Chapter 13

Outlining Your Signature Speech

Even if you are an experienced speaker, you can still find some gems in this chapter. When I talk to my clients about their delivery, I go beyond the tone, inflection, and storytelling that takes place during their speech. If you've read this far, I trust that you are a speaker who has put in the work to develop your speaking skills and your stage presence. Let's refine those skills.

In Episode 29 of my podcast, I sit down with Bob and talk to him about delivering a speech that sells. Bob is a two-time entrepreneur who typically ran workshops and seminars for other entrepreneurs. His speaking engagements were a lead generation tool, but he wanted to transition to speaking his way to cash and bringing in revenue for his speeches *as well as* gaining new clients. You can listen to the whole episode for every gem that Bob and I dropped. For now, I'll give you the highlights.

One of the biggest takeaways of the episode is the importance of developing one title for all of your presentations. At the time of the episode, Bob was creating custom presentations *every time he got on stage*. A lot of speakers do this. They practice one speech or build one PowerPoint for one audience, and they never use any of that material again. Bob identified this as a pain point, but he needed my help in overcoming that issue.

Another takeaway was the importance of controlling the energy in the room. Even when transitioning from his speech to the pitch, Bob experienced a lot of fear around "selling" to the people in his workshops. He didn't feel like he had the right message to convert people. He also didn't have an established system for following up with his audience or analyzing who was converting into a client.

You don't have to whip out your podcast app to find out what I suggested to Bob regarding these two pain points. I've got all of the information and more in this chapter. As you develop an amazing speech that you are going to deliver on stage, you will see these pain points and fears coming up over and over again. Keeping the right tools in mind, you can put those fears aside. You have done so much work preparing for this moment: putting together a system to get you in the press, assembling a six-figure package that will support your lifestyle and idea of success, and inviting clients to work with you. The groundwork has been completed. Let's talk about the service that you are going to deliver and the gifts you have to give. These gifts are worth more than money can buy. Polish them up right, and you'll find money in your pocket.

What's Your Signature Framework?

Let's go back to Bob's first pain point. He was creating *custom presentations* for every single client. That's exhausting. My suggestion to him was to develop a signature framework that he could use as the center for all his speeches. Each speech would be slightly different, but they would all adhere to one central theme.

I do this for my speeches. Do you remember "The Currency of Confidence®," the TEDx speech that I gave? This speech is based on my MBA Framework™: mindset, beliefs, and action. This framework is based on three words, but it creates plenty of opportunities to serve my clients without writing a custom speech every single time I get on stage. I bring The MBA Framework™ to many speaking engagements in front of many different audiences.

The MBA Framework™ is one of four different signature speeches that I pitch to my clients. Let's take it back a bit. Before I was delivering talks centered around The MBA Framework™, I was speaking to law students around the country about *The Law School Hustle*™. Right after I wrote *The Law School Hustle*™, I quickly realized that all of my talks to law schools would be called *The Law School Hustle*™, and the topics would be based on the chapters in my book. It was much easier than starting from scratch each time. It was a speaker's version of repurposing content. The whole framework idea is the same concept. Your framework should allow you to avoid starting from scratch when you are writing your speech.

I wrote a whole book, dropped gems, and spoke the truth about what it was really like to get the grades, get the job, and get the checks. I had *all* of this great material, and I was going to get on stage and talk about a completely different topic? No way. I realized it was much easier for me to take all of these 12 chapters and make them into 12 individual workshops. Now, these would all be subheadings for the key signature speech. For example, *The Law School Hustle: How To Brief A Case* or *The Law School Hustle: How To Network For Success.* Get it? One speech, with sub-topics based on my framework. Suddenly, I had more time on my hands. Most importantly, I was still able to deliver a phenomenal speech *because* I was using that framework that I laid out in my book, and I was not starting from scratch. I don't want you to start from scratch ever again. Do the work to create one framework that can undergird all your presentations and let that be your guiding light. That's why I love frameworks based on big creative ideas that are flexible to the audiences to whom you may speak!

I'm not telling you to read a chapter you've written word-for-word when you get on stage. I'm not saying that you deliver the same exact speech at every single engagement. Instead, revisit your framework and spend a bit of time becoming *the* expert on your topic. Every time I am booked to speak on The Currency of Confidence®, I learn something new about confidence. I've done the research. I consistently read new articles and studies about how the mind works. I know how dopamine plays a role in confidence and how your environment shapes your confidence. I understand when affirmations work and when they don't work. The only reason I know all of that is because I have had to discuss The MBA Framework™ before many different audiences. You may decide to choose one audience and stick to it. In any event, when you sit down to draft your speech, you want to start with the framework and work your way out from there.

Each time I speak on The Currency of Confidence®, I improve. My understanding of confidence deepens. I want to consistently deepen my understanding of confidence. I want to make it clear to my audience that this speech is *mine*. It's trademarked. It's based on my expertise, and I am the best person to give it. When you use The F.A.M.E. Method™ to evaluate your expertise, narrow your findings down to no more than a few topics. Boom! That's what your framework should address. That's what you need to speak on again and again until *you* are at the top of that market.

Be the Expert and Own the Market

When you have a well-developed framework to which only you can speak, you have the ability to own a piece of the market. If a company wants The Currency of Confidence®, they have one option—me or anyone who has received a license from me to give that talk. You can own the market too. That comes from developing your framework and being confident in delivering powerful presentations with it!

You don't have to write a whole book to develop a signature framework. You don't have to write a book at all if you have a signature framework! I discovered the power of using each chapter as an individual speech because I know how to leverage my time. Listen, one chapter of a book can be repurposed and used as a springboard for a new blog post, a new podcast discussion, or any number of things. Do you remember those owned media sources I talked about in Part Two? There you go. The gems you learn while researching your topic and becoming an expert will be useful as you post on social media, do interviews for podcasts, or pitch stories to the media. Look at how much you could get accomplished *just* by staying focused and having a signature framework.

Building a signature framework doesn't just save you time. The right title will establish your brand. You want your clients to know you for something. People will forget your name, but they will remember the name of your speech or framework. What are my clients going to Google after they hear me give a presentation at a conference? Will they Google my full name, Ashley Nicole Kirkwood? If they've heard from a dozen speakers that day, probably not. Are they more likely to Google "The Currency of Confidence®?" Will they search for "The P.A.I.D. Method™?" Do you think they will search "The L.O.V.E. Method™?" These are much easier to remember! The same idea applies to your signature framework.

Alright, let's get back to Bob. My suggestion to Bob was to center his brand and signature framework around the idea of "Leads Unlimited." He could name all of his speeches, workshops, and programs "Leads Unlimited" and change up the subtitles to correspond with the events he is holding and the audiences who are receiving his message. If he wanted to write a "Leads Unlimited" book, he's got a book. If he wants to trademark "Leads Unlimited," he's got that framework on lock. Every time someone heard Bob's speech even without knowing his name, they could find him through searching for "Leads Unlimited."

What is going to be the name of your speech? What are audience members and potential clients going to search when they want to reach out to you?

Writing Your Speech From Your Framework

Hopefully, I have driven home the idea that you need a framework. Let's talk about drafting your speech. We're going to talk about a basic format that I use to draft almost all speeches and workshops. If you are doing a multi-day seminar, an on-demand course, or something else, you can adjust this formula. Here it is. First, you will write out the elements of your framework. After you have the three or four elements of your framework written out, fill in the other parts of your outline like your introduction and closing thoughts.

There are several ways to start a speech, but here are some of my favorite approaches: a question, statistic, story, or study. You can use any of those, but the goal is for your approach to get the audience's attention. You have thirty seconds or less to do this.

Under each element of your framework, you will follow this format: story (personal or client story), opinion (what you think about the topic), suggestion (what you recommend), and actionable takeaways (what they can do that day or week to create a change).

Strategically, when I am just starting a speech, I like the first story to tell something personal about me to build rapport with the audience. It helps them to like you. You will also want to make sure you engage your audience. Plan out how you will engage your audience after each section of your speech. Your outline may look like this:

Introduction

- Statistic, Story, or Study
- Framework Element 1
- Story (Personal or client story)
- Opinion (What you think about the topic)
- Suggestion (What you recommend)
- Actionable Takeaways (What they can do that day or week to create a change)
- Engagement: Ask audience members to stand if the stat provided relates to them.
- Framework Element 2
- Story (Personal or client story)
- Opinion (What you think about the topic)
- Suggestion (What you recommend)
- Actionable Takeaways (What they can do that day or week to create a change)
- Engagement: Ask everyone who has ever felt _____ to raise their hands.

Framework Element 3

- Story (Personal or client story)
- Opinion (What you think about the topic)
- Suggestion (What you recommend)
- Actionable Takeaways (What they can do that day or week to create a change)
- Engagement: Ask the audience to take out their phones and text in their response to the poll displayed in the PowerPoint.

Conclusion

- Recap and thought-provoking exercise (Close your eyes and imagine…)
- Time-sensitive call to action (If you want to [INSERT RE-SULT], I want you to [text, email, tweet] me a review by midnight, and I will [incentive to provide contact information]! *You can use this strategy to collect reviews or offer to send them something you already have in exchange for them joining your list; the possibilities are endless here!*)

Control The Energy and Invite the Audience

Storytelling, tone, and inflection are cornerstones of delivering an amazing speech from the stage. They are also cornerstones for inviting clients to work with you after you step off the stage, and the event is over.

I recommend that you get really clear about the stories you are going to tell in your speech. You need to know how the story will start, who the characters are, and what the audience needs to know about them. Map it out. What will the audience feel when you are telling them a story? Always, and I mean always, end on a high note. You never want to leave your audience feeling sad.

I will never forget the time that I was in the audience, and this guy was talking about drunk driving. Apparently, he was a recovering alcoholic, and he'd previously hit someone while driving intoxicated. He started crying on stage and saying how sorry he felt about the entire situation. It was so sad. Not to mention, it didn't ever get better. He told a sad story, and he didn't give any insight into how we, the audience, could ensure that it wouldn't happen again. He did not teach us how to deal with the grief caused by such occurrences. He simply told a sad story and started crying while he was on stage. He was speaking to a group of college students and was supposed to motivate them not to drink in college. In his own way, maybe he did that, but he opened wounds on stage that he had no time to close. Do not do this. If you are talking about a serious topic, be very mindful when you share certain details and make sure you have ample time to take the audience full circle. If you don't, you can cause more harm than good.

Ideally, when you are storytelling, you have all the elements of a good story: intrigue, humor, a little drama/conflict, a moral of the story, and a happy ending. You should know what your audience will experience at each point of your story! Be sure to think through this fully! The energy you bring to the stage often will be returned to you.

If you feel sad, the audience also will feel sad. If you are excited, they will give you excited energy! Be authentic above all else but be mindful of what you are bringing to the stage!

In Bob's podcast episode, he expressed fears of "selling" to his audience. He needed a better system for giving his pitch without feeling like a used-car salesman. My advice is to control the energy in the room from the moment you get on stage to the moment you schedule your next speech. If you can control the energy in the room, you will control the energy as you transition from the meat of your speech to the invitation that you extend to clients. You won't feel awkward "selling" if you approach your speech like an invitation. If you don't feel comfortable switching your mindset from "selling" to "inviting," you have to go back and read Part Four again.

Bob was already a member of the Speak Your Way To Cash® Facebook group when he appeared on the podcast, but our conversation took him a lot closer to where he wanted to be as a speaker. He felt clarity after our coaching session and enjoyed the practical tips that I shared with him about delivering a signature speech.

As you revisit the work you did regarding The F.A.M.E. Method™ and your signature speech, I know you will find clarity too. When you commit to being an expert in *one* topic, you'll have a much easier time building a framework around that topic, delivering a confident speech, and making the transformation that you want to see in others.

Now, after you have your outline ready, it's time to practice your speech. I personally don't write my speech out word for word. I practice my speech based on my outline. I write out the research points I need to memorize, and I write individual outlines for the stories I will use in my speeches. I practice speeches 5-10 times before I give a presentation live. Practice as much as you need to in order to feel comfortable!

Here's some things to remember from this chapter:

- Make sure you base your speeches on your framework. That is your guide to everything.

- Ensure you outline your speech, so it's clear and impactful for the audience.

- Be sure to engage your audience during your presentation.

- Practice your speech until you feel comfortable.

Act Your Way to Cash™

Take a video of you giving your speech. Don't worry if it's not perfect. You're not going to send this to potential clients. If you speak to sell, which means you use speaking as a way to sell your products primarily, be sure to include your pitch in the recording. Play it back. What do you notice about your tone or your inflection? How does your energy change or stay the same throughout the speech? If you want extra feedback, reach out to me via email to set up a VIP Day! Email me at ashley@speakyourwaytocash.com!

Chapter 14

Delivering An Amazing Speech Virtually

I wrote this book at the height of the COVID-19 pandemic. All of my presentations in 2020 and most of my presentations in 2021 were virtual. I learned quite a bit about how to present virtually. Even before the pandemic, however, I had given more than 100 virtual talks. Let's discuss how you can keep an audience engaged virtually. Virtual speeches require you to prepare differently, but they can be an amazing opportunity in 2021 and beyond.

Engage!

You already know that speaking on a stage and speaking virtually are different. I see a lot of advantages to speaking virtually. I can avoid traveling away from my husband and daughter, and ending the engagement is as easy as logging off. However, there are drawbacks to speaking virtually too. These drawbacks aren't anything that you or I can't handle, though. You still can deliver an amazing speech!

The biggest difference between speaking on stage and speaking virtually is the ability or inability to *engage with the crowd*. It's easy for me to get onstage and woo everyone in the audience. I can see people's faces. I read their facial expressions, and their body language isn't "hidden." In an auditorium, I can tell everyone to stand up, sit down, raise their hands, or catch prizes that I throw out into the crowd. (All of that happens at my in-person speaking events, and it should happen at your events too.) However, what happens if you have a virtual audience and all their cameras are off? What happens if there's no engagement at all? You may not be able to "see" your audience. That changes things. You may have to incentivize engagement, as we will discuss that later in this chapter.

Be sure to engage with the audience intentionally. Plan to engage with the audience every two to three slides. Have them type answers and echo your thoughts in the chat. Host polls. Give everyone a number to text. Put people in breakout sessions. Encourage people to send private messages to people they know and tell them something they have learned so far in the presentation. Not only do you have to plan to engage with the audience, but your engagement needs some diversity. Don't have them put the same word in the chat over and over. Tell people to stand up wherever they are or turn their cameras off and then on again. Do whatever you can to keep your audience's attention and plan for it.

Right off the bat, you have to set expectations that you are going to engage with the audience. You can do that through your words *and* your actions. Anyone who isn't on camera should not be visible. Bring engaged audience members to the forefront. Here's a little something that I like to do in virtual presentations. At the beginning of a speech, I will let the audience know that I have a "bonus" word for them. I tell them that at the end of the speech, if they send me the bonus word in a text message or the chat, I'll send them a gift. During one of my slides, I will flash a bonus word on the screen and award a prize to the person who sends it to me first! You don't have to use this technique. Find something creative that reflects your brand and keeps the audience engaged.

I use the same kind of incentive to encourage audience members to fill out the post-event survey. My audience knows that I will pick three people who filled out the survey and send them a physical copy of my book!

Plan, Plan, Plan

I'm going to let you know just *how* much you have to plan when you're speaking virtually. (Spoiler alert: You have to plan *a lot.*) Planning every time you raise your voice or encouraging people to text a response will *feel* tedious, but it will keep people engaged. Also, don't underestimate your tone of voice. Sometimes, you need to whisper a "secret" to the audience or say something much louder. You may need to do voice impersonations when you are telling a story. You want to bring your presentation to life. Think about how you want to switch it up. Here's a truth bomb. Most people don't pay me to speak; they pay me to per-form. They want me to provide an experience. Here is my roadmap to planning an amazing virtual speech.

Plan Your Tone and Inflection

I like to start my presentations with an icebreaker to get people laughing and set expectations for the experience. As you plan your speech, you want to be clear about when you're going to raise your voice, when you're going to keep your voice soft, and when you're going to pause. You have to plan when you're going to bring someone else into the conversation, when you're going to stop and think, and when you're going to grab a sip of water. Plan it all, so *you* can control the energy in the virtual "room" better. Controlling the energy in the room is crucial to delivering an amazing speech in person, but this task is much harder when everyone is in a separate location. Think about every moment. Plan it and write it down.

Have Your Talking Points Ready

Everything needs to be in your talking points, and your talking points need to look like a chart with three columns. On the left side of my talking points, I have the slide number that corresponds to my presentation. In the middle, I have my talking points and any notes I have about tone and inflection. On the right side, I include infor-mation about any workbook pages or activity sheets that I'm going to direct the audience to complete. If I'm going off the PowerPoint, I put the moment I'm going off the slides and mark the place where I'm returning to my talking points. For example:

Slide #	Talking Points	Interaction/Notes
1	**Introduction Slide** • Describe who you are and how many years you have in the industry. Set the tone for the presentation. • Announce the bonuses they get for active participation. • Remember to smile. • Let them know how we will use the digital companion guide during the presentation	Pull up the first poll.
2	**Who is in the audience?** • Get a feel for who is in the audience. • What countries/states are present?	Ask them to drop their city in the chat.

Everything goes in my talking points, and I keep those talking points close by while I'm speaking virtually. When I am speaking in-person, I may have a notecard, but I don't remember the last time I physically held notes while I was talking. If I want the audience to text me, engage with each other, or move into breakout rooms, I have that all in my talking points. Any videos or clips that I include in my speech, I include in my talking points. (Hot tip: I keep clips to 15-30 seconds to keep the audience engaged.)

This preparation is critical. Why? If a corporate client is paying you $5,000 or $15,000 to give a virtual presentation, they need to know that you're legit. You do this for real. You don't just go onto Canva before the presentation and throw some stuff together. Your clients don't want you to do that, and you don't want to do that either. You are excellent, and that's the standard you want your clients to see. Don't say I never complimented you before. Ha!

Plan for Technical Difficulties

Your talking points also should have *alternatives* in case videos don't work, or the audio goes out. If your video doesn't play, what are you going to do? If the video plays but the audio doesn't play, what are you going to do? We all know that technology can be fickle and doesn't play by our rules all the time. Prepare alternatives in case something does not go according to your plan.

One thing that I do is include links to multimedia clips in the workbooks that I provide to attendees. All that information is there for them to follow along. If videos don't play or my connection is bad, I tell the audience that they can head to page X, Y, or Z of their workbook and play the multimedia clip on their own time. I tell them once they've watched it to send me a text or email message after the presentation and let me know what they think.

You always have to plan for the worst case scenario. Have a back-up platform if your tech platform of choice is acting up. Make sure your audience can access the event from the computer or their phone. I don't know what date you're reading this book, so I can't guarantee that platforms that I use will be around (we have used Zoom, Hopin, LiveWebinar, etc.). Find alternative platforms and have them ready to go in case your first platform experiences technical difficulties.

Talk to the Client and an Audience Member Beforehand

As I'm putting my talking points together, I reach out to the client. We typically have a final call at least two weeks before the event. During that call, I ask a series of questions that help me understand the audience better and identify what last-minute touches I can add to the presentation. I ask the client what they enjoyed about past virtual presentations and what felt like a drag to them. I asked them about the biggest issues they have been facing on the topics about which I've been hired to speak. I ask them what else I need to know about the audience that I may not have asked already.

Most importantly, I use this call as a way to gauge the energy of the audience. By the end of 2020, most people were exhausted from virtual presentations. I addressed this in the beginning of my speech and set expectations for myself and the audience. When audience members were exhausted, I reassured them that if they stuck with me, they would love the experience. I promised them that I would be engaged. Do not be afraid to address the elephants in the rooms and the fatigue that your audience members may be feeling in *or* after the COVID-19 pandemic. Use this opportunity to build a connection and start your speech off on the right foot.

During the call with the client, I send over any workbooks that the audience will need and any other materials that will be important for marketing the event. I also ask whether I can speak with someone who will be in the audience. If I am speaking to a group of students, I ask to speak with a student beforehand. If I am speaking to a group of biologists, I ask to speak with a biologist from the company beforehand. This is important because the person who hires me is oftentimes not a representative of the audience to whom I will be speaking. Your audience and your client are not always the same. You sell to your client, but you want to make sure you do a great job presenting to the audience. I do a pre-event call with the client *and* a pre-event call with an audience member. I want to know what the audience member is going through, what is a struggle for them, and what I can add to my presentation that will resonate with them. In addition to speaking with your client and a member of the audience, be sure to test out your technology beforehand.

Work With Your Team to Build Engagement

Do you see why I have a framework for all of my speeches? I do not want to spend time writing an entirely new speech *and* putting together detailed talking points. The way that I prepare for speeches has made my services more profitable and adaptable when things go wrong. When you plan to deliver your speech, consider how you will prepare to make your presentation a success.

Having a team helps. They make sure my PowerPoints are right, and my workbooks are ready to send. I hire instructional designers to put together my talking points and conduct research. I also instruct them to include prompts for engagement every few slides. Of course, I'm not letting them *guess* what engagement I'm going to plan. As a speaker, you are the expert in the presentation you are putting together. You know the modalities you are going to use to engage with the audience. You are the one having the call with the client. You know the preferred learning style of your audience better than your instructional designers. You have to walk your team through each part of the presentation and let them know your vision for the presentation.

Instructional designers cut down on your prep time, but you give them the material. I typically have a recorded call with my instructional designer and go over all the content and direct them on what to research. I tell them what stats I need, and they use the recording to craft the speech. Having a signature framework for your speeches will cut down on your prep time. In this new era of virtual events, finding opportunities to speak virtually will cut down on certain elements of your prep time *and* your travel time. These opportunities are everywhere. All you need to do is find them, prepare for them, and deliver.

Below are some things to remember from this chapter:

- You need to prepare thoroughly for each presentation and make sure you have well-laid-out talking points.

- Be sure to engage often and diversely. There are plenty of engagement ideas in this chapter.

- Have a team to help you prepare. They can be contractors, but you want to make sure your presentation is well researched and designed.

- Talk to your client and a member of the audience before your engagement to ensure your presentation will be a success.

Act Your Way to Cash™

Take out your notebook and draft your virtual event standard operating procedures. What platform will you use? What's your backup platform? How far in advance will you do your tech run-through? When will you set up your polls and interactions? Who will engage in the chat during your virtual presentations? Prepare this now, so once you land the engagement, you know exactly what to do!

Chapter 15

Delivering a Great Customer Experience

To be a highly paid speaker, not only do you need to deliver a great speech, but also you need to have great customer service! Don't get so wrapped up in the technical details that you forget about your customers' entire client experience journey! You cannot, and I repeat, cannot, have incredible customer service if the underlying service is trash. It simply can't happen. The primary responsibility of a service provider is to provide an incredible underlying product. If you promise your speech will teach three things, then you need to teach three things. If you promise to show your client areas where they can improve productivity, do that and track it! Always have a way to measure the success of your service! In the last section, we explored how to deliver an amazing speech. Let's discuss how to deliver incredible customer service.

Getting a new client once is not the ultimate goal! We want forever clients. Why? Well, check this out. Did you know that:

- It's five times more expensive to acquire a new customer than retaining one that you have.[5]

- If you increase customer retention by just 5%, studies show that you can increase profits anywhere from 5-95%.[6]

- Loyal customers are 5 times more likely than new customers to forgive you when mistakes happen.[7]

- It is reported that U.S. companies lose $136.8 billion dollars per year (whoa!) due to avoidable customer-switching costs![8]

Did that convince you that you need to focus on customer service? I hope so! Here's what I want you to do. Write a list in a Google Sheet of every single last one of your speaking clients from last year who were free or paid and note the following:

- Their name

- The date they booked you

- The amount they paid

- They way you acquired the client

- Their email

- An internal customer rating

- Their address

- Their birthday

- Their favorite candy/treat

Then, I want you to develop a customer retention plan for them. Most of those categories are self-explanatory, but I want you to make sure you note how you acquired the client. This will tell you where you found the client. If you found the client from a referral, note that. If they saw an ad, note that. The other category on which I want to elaborate is the "internal customer rating." You need to note whether you like working with these clients in this column. You can do this a couple of ways; we have three categories: dream, good fit, and standard. Dream clients are the clients we would take any day, every day. They are amazing to work with and they have strong values. Good fit clients are great to work with but don't have as many opportunities for us to serve them. Standard clients are okay to work with, but they either (a) don't pay on time; (b) aren't 100% a good fit from a values perspective; (c) don't follow our processes; or (d) don't have an ample amount of work for us to serve them. You can rate your clients in any way you see fit, but this works for us!

After you have this Excel sheet filled out, you can get to work. What is your retention plan for these clients? How often are you communicating with them? I would recommend you touch base on the low end once per month and contact them on their birthday, Christmas, and New Year's Day. Do you know when they get budgetary approval? If so, make that a column as well and reach out to them around that time too. People know you are in business to make money, but clients like to feel that you want their business. They want to feel special.

What types of gifts are good for clients' birthdays and holidays?

Birthdays:

- Custom notebooks and pens if they are really nice

- Custom popcorn with a nice message on it

- Self-care boxes

- Custom flowers in the client's brand colors

- Other branded items

Don't overthink this. If you know what they like, get them that! You can get them a gift card to their favorite restaurant or something else you know they'll enjoy. Here's a caveat that you may need to consider; some clients (government, state officials, etc.) may have gift rules that prevent them from accepting gifts over a certain amount, so I typically have gone with a standard gift for all clients of a similar nature, so there's no appearance of impropriety. When you are in doubt, ask the clients. They will appreciate that. A simple note like the following is good.

Hey John. Each year, we send our clients a token of our appreciation around the holidays! Some of our clients have rules about accepting small gifts. Is there anything we should be aware of when we are adding you to our holiday mailing list? We just want to be respectful, but we also want to let you know we're thinking of you!

That is simple and easy. Just ask them. Then, you want to make sure you are doing a direct ask quarterly for business or referrals. This is critical. The gifts are great, and not each gift should come with an ask, but you should ask directly for business or referrals quarterly.

Here's how you can do this.

Hey John. I just thought about you today and wanted to drop you a note. We are currently planning our fall client calendar, and we would love to serve you again! Are you looking for ways to increase employee engagement currently? I know last time we spoke, you noted that there were some new managers starting who might benefit from the AIM Method™. Do you have any time to touch base on this next week?

P.S. Do you have any colleagues in the industry who I should know? I have enjoyed working with you and would love to be connected with more like-minded people!

Best,

Do you see how short and to-the-point that was? For those of you reading this with past clients, I want you to email all of them to see if (a) they have any needs; and (b) they have anyone to whom they can refer you! You can edit the script above if needed!

Customer Mapping

What is your customer's journey from start to finish? Do you know? If you don't know, you need to draw out a customer map. This will help you to visualize your customer's experience and know where you need to make improvements. Here's an example:

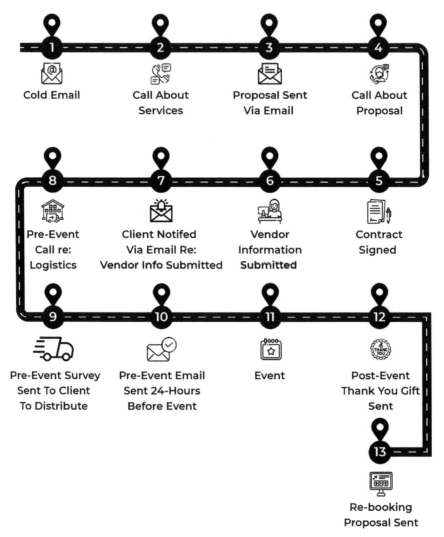

1. Cold Email
2. Call About Services
3. Proposal Sent Via Email
4. Call About Proposal
5. Contract Signed
6. Vendor Information Submitted
7. Client Notifed Via Email Re: Vendor Info Submitted
8. Pre-Event Call re: Logistics
9. Pre-Event Survey Sent To Client To Distribute
10. Pre-Event Email Sent 24-Hours Before Event
11. Event
12. Post-Event Thank You Gift Sent
13. Re-booking Proposal Sent

© 2021 Speak Your Way To Cash ®

This is just a portion of a customer map for a customer who books a keynote speech. When a client books a long-term speaking/consulting contract, this may look very different! We may have monthly calls, quarterly deep-dive sessions, and a lot more check-ins for feedback! However, let's look at this map for a minute! Do you see the organized check-in process? When you are selling a client on working with you and you have a process, you can walk the client through exactly what will happen when they purchase from you. They will have no ambiguity about that—none! That certainty builds trust, which is exactly what you want to build.

After you write out your process, you need to think, *What can I do to make the client feel appreciated after each step?* When the client signs the contract, instead of just an email, you could send a handwritten note. This can even be automated! Look up a few handwritten note tools that integrate with your CRM to get this done! We use Handwrytten to send out handwritten notes! With so much happening via email, personalization and sending things in the mail (besides bills) are welcomed! You also could send a branded welcome box with items the client actually can use in it! All of our U.S.-based Speak Your Way To Cash® Live attendees get something in the mail from us! Think about how you can create a WOW factor at each stage of the process!

How to Be Consistently Booked

If you have heard Episode 84 of the podcast, you might know what I'm about to say. I talked about the *one* thing you need to do that is more important than selling. Here's what I have to say about that:

The #1 thing that consistently booked speakers do is they ensure that they do not stop the relationship after they provide the deliverable.

This is a huge mistake that I see speakers make all the time. They think that when the event is over, their job is done. Your job is not done! Yes, the customer has made their way down the "sales funnel," but funnels only go one direction. Thinking of the customer journey as a never-ending circle puts more money in your pocket. Don't let the relationship end after one engagement. Circle back *every time.*

I didn't always do this. I booked one-time speeches and didn't follow up, and I always started the month "at zero." Every month, I felt like I had to start my process over again to book clients. I was scrambling, and I didn't want to scramble. By implementing a system that took my clients on a circular journey, I never started the month at zero. I was booked consistently. I knew when money was coming into my pocket. When I started seeing a rebooking rate of 80%, I could breathe more easily. Getting the "yes" became easier.

This is the only approach that will get you booking after booking, month after month. You have to ask for referrals and re-engage with clients who already know you, love you, and see the value in your work. This is how you build long-term relationships. How do you re-engage with your clients? You have to ensure that after each and every event you have a follow-up call!

The Follow-Up Call

Don't worry. I'm going to walk you through each step of the follow-up call, including what to say.

Schedule it before you speak.

During your pre-event call, which takes place two weeks before your speech, you will want to schedule the post-event call. Scheduling that call feels like planning too far ahead, but trust me, when the client is on the phone with you *before* the event, they're excited. They'll commit to the follow-up call. More importantly, they'll go through with it. Once the event is over, you're going to have a much harder time scheduling a call. Your client already has the next week or next month planned out. It is better to put your call on the calendar before it's too late. You might have to reschedule but put that call on the calendar.

Gather your own feedback.

Here's a pro tip for speakers. There are two "customers" who you are serving. Yes, you're scheduling the follow-up call with the client who made the decision to book you. That person is not your only customer. The *other* customers are the people in the audience, and both customers will have feedback about the event whether you ask them for it or not.

What I'm saying is that your client is going to hear from your audience about your speech. You have to be in on that conversation. You have to gather that data and collect that feedback yourself. Do you remember in the Invite section when I told you about the survey I sent out after hosting an event based on *The Law School Hustle*™? You have to send out a similar survey to get this information back from your audience.

You have to have a system for gathering that feedback and having enough data to present to your client on your follow-up call. You have to make the collection of feedback and data part of your process. It should be on your customer map.

Give your client permission to give you feedback.

Let's talk about what happens on the actual follow-up call. You finally get on the call, and you have feedback and data ready to share with your client, but you also want to get feedback from them. Hold off on the data for a second and just have a conversation with them.

First, you're going to find out what went well. What did your client like about the presentation? Which tools were helpful? What was the most enjoyable part of the process for your client and their audience? Get this information first. Clients usually feel more comfortable sharing compliments before critiques. Let the compliments roll in first.

You will want to talk about what you can do better. As a speaker, you always can change and improve your performance. I know that even after giving my *Law School Hustle* presentation dozens of times to thousands of law students, I can make some improvements and make the engagement more impactful.

Here's the thing about feedback, though. Not all clients feel comfortable talking about the not-so-great parts of your speech. When you get on that call, you have to give your client *permission* to give you feedback. I love getting feedback, and I let my clients know that on every follow-up call. If you don't give permission to your clients explicitly, you might not hear what they have to say, or you may not learn what you can do to improve your speech and deliver a better service.

The call doesn't stop there! Your client is going to have more good things to say than "bad" things. Once you have gathered all the feedback from the engagement, circle back to the good stuff. Ask for feedback or testimonials that you can use on your website or in other marketing materials. Ask for feedback on what other organizations or colleagues may be a good fit for the products and services you deliver. These small asks will help you elevate your brand and make pitching new clients a *much* easier process.

Figure out your next steps.

Once you've collected feedback, it's time to figure out the next steps. Check in about the future of the organization and the future of the client's position in the organization. People get promoted. Companies may change their vision in the wake of a pandemic, an acquisition, or leadership changes. Gather this information before you propose next steps.

By this point of the call, you have so much information that you can use to invite the client to work with you *again*. At this point, you may bring up the feedback you received from the survey you administered. You may revisit the vision you co-created during your original call. This is the time when you discuss your next steps and work toward closing a new deal.

We're in a circle, right? You might feel like you're back at the start of your pitching journey, but in reality, you are miles ahead of the competition. You already delivered an amazing speech. You developed a relationship with the client, and you are just one signature away from closing another deal. This is why treating customer maps like a circle is so important. You save a heck of a lot of time rebooking a client than going back to your CRM, finding a potential client, and picking up the phone to pitch your services and introduce yourself. On a feedback call, the introduction is *done*. You just have to pitch.

Track your data.

My goal is to rebook three out of every five clients I speak with on a follow-up call. How are you going to know if you're doing that without tracking your data? I talk to a lot of speakers who do not have a way of tracking their conversion metrics. You have to collect that data to determine the value of your engagements and identify where you can improve!

After each and every follow-up call, update your CRM. Did your client book another engagement? Do they need you to follow up in a week, a month, or six months? Have they received a proposal for a long-term package? Even if the client says, "no," you have opportunities to track data and gain valuable information from the follow-up call. Do not miss out on that opportunity!

Look for Opportunities in the "No" or "Not Yet"

Pitching your client during the follow-up call does give your client the opportunity to say "yes," "no," or "not yet."

Uncover the objections.

Look, people change jobs all the time. Budgets change. Responsibilities change. The "objection" to your pitch may not be about you at all! If your client is not interested in rebooking, you have to circle back to the vision and the future that you discussed with the client. Is the person to whom you are talking the person who will make decisions about speakers and events in the future? Is that person changing positions or jobs? Where can you fit into this future?

If you can partner with your client at their current company or elsewhere, you have an opportunity to continue working with them. If you build a future where you partner with the company through your current contact or one of their colleagues, you have an opportunity to continue working with that company. Either way, you need information to grow the relationship so ask for it! You are going to need these objections as data anyway so don't be afraid to dig deep.

Add them to your marketing materials.

If the client is not subscribed to your newsletter already, get their permission to do so. Do you have a new podcast episode out that the client can enjoy? Send them a link after the follow-up call. Leave your

client with something of value just like you would if they were a potential client who turned down your initial pitch.

Getting this permission gives you the opportunity to continue
the conversation. Add them to an email sequence written just for clients who you want to rebook. Schedule a monthly or quarterly check-
in on your CRM. Until they say "no," you are still in the process of
pitching. Even when they do say "no," they might say "yes" to email
sequences, newsletters, and other marketing materials that keep you at
the front of their mind.

What have you gained?

A Speak Your Way To Cash® speaker finds opportunities even
in the face of objections. Look at everything you have gained and
learned from the speaking engagement. How many connections have
you made? What lessons have you learned? What relationships have
you built? These are the places where you can find opportunities to
build your speaking career and deliver a better customer experience
for the next client. Look for those opportunities and track that data!

Here are some key points to remember from this chapter:
- You should always ask for referrals. That's a key way for you
  to get more clients.
- You must have a follow-up call after your event and schedule
  it before your event.
- Be sure to collect your own feedback and present the data you
  collected to the client to assist in the rebooking conversation.

Act Your Way to Cash™

Take a look at your CRM. Have you included clients with whom you have worked in the past? Follow up with three previous clients to check in for a quick chat. Use this opportunity to ask them for references or referrals. Then, make a plan for following up with them again next month or next quarter. Keep those relationships alive!

Part Six

Get P.A.I.D!

Chapter 16

Legalities That Every Speaker Should Consider

Did you think I was going to write a whole book and not include anything about the law? By now, you know that I founded a law firm, Mobile General Counsel®, and I see first-hand why speakers and business owners need to lawyer up. Even if you do not have a lawyer on retainer every month, you should consider some of the legalities that will protect your content and your business. You have worked too hard throughout the journey of reading this book to have your business stolen. If you have a signature speech, an online course, or any other type of content that is solely yours, protect it.

What Could Go Wrong?

The answer to that question is anything could go wrong. We serve a lot of entrepreneurs including speakers and consultants at Mobile General Counsel®. I've seen it all. Speakers have come to me looking to trademark their signature speech only to find out someone has trademarked it already. If someone has trademarked your signature speech, you may have to change the name of your speech, or worse. You could be sued for infringement and requested to pay the trademark owner money. In some cases, trademark owners can ask for all the money you've made using the name that they own and then some. This stuff can get messy and expensive. Protecting yourself on the legal side may feel like it's optional, but it's actually essential.

I could write a whole book on the horror stories that come out of failing to protect your business. I can't give you specifics (for obvious reasons), but I can tell you that I've seen people try to steal trademarks from other people. I have seen lawsuits filed over someone stealing another person's work, and years of work were flushed down the drain because someone did not take the steps to protect their brand properly. Don't even get me started on contract negotiations!

Here's the truth. Are you ready for the truth? *All* business owners need legal protections, and speakers are included in that group. You have put so much work into your brand. You have pitched your brand to the press, put together a six-figure package, invited clients to work with you, and delivered an amazing speech that transforms lives. It would be terrible to see someone use all of your hard work to make a profit for themselves. Legal protections ensure that you get paid for your work, and they ensure that you are the only one who gets paid for the work you put into developing your unique brand.

If you are serious about making money from speaking, you have to consider legally protecting yourself and your brand. This is a process with a few moving parts including contracts, copyrights, and trademarks. Are you using contracts, copyrights, and trademarks to protect your business? If you're not, don't worry. I'm going to break these down and show you why you have to start bringing them into your business. This is at least a portion of what you need to know if you are considering taking the first steps to protect your business and your content.

First, let me give you a disclaimer. Nothing in this section is an attempt to form an attorney-client relationship, and it is only used for educational purposes. Now that the disclaimer is out of the way, let's dive in.

Contracts

First things first, let's talk about contracts. Before you reach out to a client or before you consider trademarks, get your contracts in order. Why? It is simple. Contracts protect your coins. They tell everyone who will do what, when, and for how much. They also should be really clear about who owns what. That piece is critical.

Speaking engagements don't look the same as they did in 2019. Live events were canceled in 2020. In-person events were switched to virtual events, and disputes took place over the value of events in this "new normal." Does a client get a refund if their Zoom stops working? Do they expect to pay less if an event is no longer in-person? What happens when the Wi-Fi glitches in the middle of the presentation? Who owns the recorded content? Does the speaker or the company own that material? This is a biggie. So many speakers lose money on their engagements because they don't have contracts, or they sign contracts that allow their clients to own all of their intellectual property.

Your contracts should answer all of these questions and more. Handshakes and confirmation emails don't mean as much as you think. You have to have the engagement, your payment, and other agreements memorialized in writing. Cancellation policies look different in a virtual landscape, but they might vary between a client and a speaker. Contracts ensure that you are both on the same page. What can you both expect in case of a glitch, a cancellation, or a rescheduled event? Who owns the intellectual property? Can they replay the recorded presentation without paying you each time? How long can they do this? What happens if they pay late? Is there a late fee? If you go to court, who pays what costs? What happens if you fall off the stage during an event and accidentally fall on an attendee? Are you liable for that? Are they liable? What are your insurance requirements? It's a lot!

What goes in a contract?

Contracts can be made between two or more people for almost anything as long as it's legal. The enforceability of the contract typically is determined based on state law, the contract itself, and a judge's interpretation of the agreement.

Your contract should address at least the following elements, but this is a non-exhaustive list:

- Identification of the Parties

- Terms of the Agreement

- Payment

- Intellectual Property (IP) Ownership

- Confidentiality

- Licensing

- Indemnity

- Choice of Law/Venue

- Severability

- Late Payment

- Cancellation

There are also several other provisions that our firm includes to make sure that our clients are protected. The attorneys at Mobile General Counsel® draft a mean agreement.

If you are worried about what happens if you can't perform the contract for reasons outside your control, you can add what's called a force majeure clause or an Acts of God clause. This clause can serve to free you and your client from any obligations or liabilities in case of an unforeseen event outside of either party's control. This clause may cover things such as lightning strikes, severe storms, crimes, sudden legal changes, or a global pandemic. Your agreement should define what is covered and what is excluded. You are not restricted to what I have listed here. This is a common clause in contracts, so your clients will not be offended to see it in writing. If you have talked about specific agreements like what happens if the power goes out, you can add this into the contract too. Do not forget that force majeure clause. It needs to be well drafted.

Also, let me say this. If you have to go at it alone, the one provision you need to read closely is the IP provision. You need to know who owns your content. As a speaker, that's your most valuable asset. Your speech is your IP. If a client wants to own that, they need to pay you handsomely. Instead of just giving a client the rights to watch and replay your presentation at will, sell them a non-exclusive license to the replay of your presentation. Leverage your IP.

Do not be afraid to send over a contract. Ideally, you would send them your contract that you've had expertly drafted by an attorney. A lot of speakers feel strange sending over a contract with strict clauses to big companies. Don't feel strange. Don't be afraid to draw up or sign a contract. You aren't likely going to lose a deal if you send over terms and conditions. Corporations are used to signing contracts. They often take so long booking a speaker because they want to draw up a contract or adhere to other contracts they have signed!

If you feel uncomfortable drawing up a contract, reach out to a lawyer. We have renegotiated and drafted contracts for clients and helped them get hundreds of thousands of dollars more out of deals because of them. If you know that you would like your lawyer to draft and negotiate your contract, in the rate discussion, be sure to note, "*Our packages typically start at* _____, *but the final costs depend on the particulars of the contract.*" Leave yourself some room to grow the engagement on the pricing side, so your lawyer can swoop in and help you get more out of the deal—if they're good. Your lawyer then can put the contract together and send it out. Remember, contracts are in place to protect you. Even the most upstanding corporations can give you a contract with terms that are excellent for them, but bad for you. Have your contract reviewed by an attorney. Protect yourself. In some cases, you can sign a contract, put it in a desk, and never look at it again. However, if things go south, you'll be happy that you have a strongly worded agreement that protects you.

Copyrights

Contracts are pretty routine. Most likely, you already have signed one or sent one out to a client. We're going to get into some more good stuff. If you are a serious speaker, you have to start thinking about copyrights and trademarks.

Here's the difference. Copyrights protect creative work or content, and trademarks protect commercial names, logos or slogans. There's more to it than that, obviously, but at a base level, that should help you get an idea of which protection you need. My book has a copyright, and we filed for a federal trademark for The P.A.I.D. Method™. For now, let's get into copyrights.

As a speaker, you will find yourself sharing creative work to promote your brand or just sharing your gifts with the world. Maybe you write a book filled with your expertise. You build an online course to educate clients further on your signature speech. You write guest blogs based on the work you have done throughout your speaking career. Podcasts, coaching programs, and online quizzes are all forms of creative work that can help you monetize your gifts. If these creative works aren't protected, they're vulnerable. People can steal chapters from your book and claim them as their own. They can repost your podcast recordings on their website and make a profit. They can steal an online quiz and give it to their employees without paying you a dime. That's not the way that you monetize your gifts. If you want to monetize your gifts and bring revenue into your business, you have to protect your creative works by registering them with the United States Federal Copyright Office.

Here's what happens if you file a federal copyright application to protect your work. People are going to see that your work should be taken seriously. When your work is credited by clients, more people will be directed to your creative work and become familiar with your brand. If you see someone using your words or audio without permission, you can take that person to court. If you don't have a federally registered copyright, you will have a tough time proving ownership and collecting money when someone steals your work. While it is true that you have some rights as soon as the work is created to protect it and collect money for the theft, registering your creations with the United States Federal Copyright Office is the way to go.

Obtaining a copyright for your business can take up to six months, if not longer, but that process will be worth the moment of relief when you see another person trying to use your work, and you know that you can take action at the federal level.

I may have said this before, but the way that you say "thank you" in America is with a check. If a client loves your work, they prove it by paying you for it. Similarly, the way that you say "sorry" in America is also with a check. Here's what I mean; when someone commits a crime against you like a theft, etc., they can go to jail. Additionally, you have the right to sue them in civil court for money depending on several factors. Jail is a criminal penalty. When someone steals from you or commits a wrong against you in business, they don't typically go to jail unless a crime also was involved. What do you do? You sue them for damages. Damages is a fancy way that we say money in the legal world. The way you say "sorry" is with a check. There are two systems: the criminal justice system and the civil system. When someone commits a wrong against your business, you go after them using the civil justice system, and you ask for money. If you don't have your documents and federal registrations in order, however, the law limits your ability to recoup money for the wrong that was committed against you. Does that make sense?

Whew. I had to put my law professor hat on for a minute. Let's chat about trademarks.

Trademarks

The first thing I did when I opened Mobile General Counsel® was apply for a trademark. No one else would be able to operate under that name and make money off the work that I put into building my practice and serving my clients. If someone wanted to work with Mobile General Counsel®, that person was going to work with *me*.

As a speaker, I obtained trademarks for my signature speeches, brand name, and even specific methodologies that I use as frameworks for different creative works. I have a trademark on Speak Your Way To Cash® because Speak Your Way To Cash® is a commercial name that I use for my brand and my products. The P.A.I.D. Method™ is the name of a methodology that I use in signature speeches, in my book, and at the center of *many* live training sessions. The L.O.V.E. Method™ and The Currency of Confidence® are names that are associated with my brand. When people search "The Currency of Confidence®," they find my speech.

Trademarks help clients identify your brand and your company name. When you are thinking about applying for a trademark, think about how you plan on making money in the future. What names are going to bring in the cash? What slogans do you want people to associate with *you* and your brand? What is going to make you money in the future? Those names are what you want to trademark. This is where understanding your expertise really comes into play. By the end of the chapter, you'll see that building a strategy around trademarks and other legalities will help you elevate your business. Knowing what *and when* to trademark your signature framework will help to guide the direction of your business.

When should you get your brand name trademarked? You should do this early. I tell my speaking clients that they have a few tasks they have to accomplish if they want to protect their brand from the get-go. The first thing they need to do is get their contracts in order. Secondly, they need to file federal trademark applications for all brand names, logos, and slogans used in their business. Most brands wait until they are selling goods under their brand name to get a trademark, *but* you can apply for a trademark even earlier. If you know that you are going to use your trademark in commerce within a few months of getting your trademark, get that process started.

There's a special application that will allow you to apply for a trademark even before you start using the name! Obviously, before your name is registered, you have to show proof of use, but you don't have to wait to file! Get started! Obtaining a trademark can take *at least* 10 months, but it also can take a year or longer. The time is worth it, though. Trademarks can last *forever* if you keep up with the additional required filings after you secure your name! Do you want to file your own federal trademark application? Head to *ashleynicolekirkwood.shop* to grab my DIY trademarks class, Get The Tea On Trademarks™! I do not recommend DIY'ing it unless you can't afford a lawyer but do what you have to do*!*

About Licensing

Having your content copyrighted and trademarked isn't just about legal protection. These legalities also tie into the assembly of your package. Yes, that's right. We're going back to section three! Do you remember that long list of product and service offerings from that chapter? (If you don't, go back and check it out. I'll be here.) Licensing is on there. If you own your signature speech, you can license it out. If you own a training, you can license it out. I'm talking about licensing out your content for six months or a year in exchange for five figures. When you have your legalities right, you can add income to your business.

Anything you own, you can license out. You can license your image if you want! Let me say this again, so you remember it as you revisit your packages. Anything you own, you can license out. Clients may attend a virtual event and call you two weeks later asking you to send over a replay. Nope! If you license out your speeches, you can send the client's entire team a replay for a fee—a licensing fee, to be exact. For three months, six months, or a year, your client will have access to your speech, course, or whatever you want to license out to them. After time runs out, they can renew the license for a five-figure fee.

Speakers approach licensing in a few different ways. Some speakers make one speech and license it out to all their clients across the country. Other speakers create a package and give a client exclusive rights to that package (for a much higher fee). Fees may be determined by a flat rate, the number of people who get access to your content, or the length of time the content is available to the client. Do not miss out on the opportunity to get compensation for the work you did to put together your speech and record it for others to use!

Meet Rashad Rayford

Speakers run into situations all the time in which they could be coaxed into undervaluing their work and giving away their gifts for a low, low price. Take Rashad Rayford. Rashad is a poet. He has been in the game for 20 years. In the past four years or so, he has blended spoken word poetry with speaking to create an exciting, innovative brand called Elevate Your Vibe, LLC. Check him out. He's amazing.

Rashad connected with me on Facebook a few years ago. He's worked with coaches before, and he was not new to the speaking game when he first tuned into the podcast or attended one of my week-long classes. However, learning about copyrights, trademarks, and licensing tightened up his business and helped him get a clear focus of what he wanted to do, where he wanted to go, and when he was going to walk away from deals that undervalued his gifts.

In January 2021, Rashad connected with a corporation that was based in Los Angeles. They wanted him to do an hour-long keynote speech and a 15-minute Q&A session. When Rashad started talking to the potential client about money, he realized their budget was all wrong. He had done his research and knew this corporation could pay him *much* more than they were offering. This was not good. Rashad also knew that because he was giving this speech on a digital platform, he had to ask questions about intellectual property and inquire how his work was going to be protected.

Here's where things got wild. The potential employee told Rashad initially that his speech would be viewed by 1,000 employees.

After Rashad asked about intellectual property, the client let it slip that the speech would be shown *again* to another 4,000-5,000 employees around the world. His speech would be shown to over 6,000 employees around the world, and they were trying to pay him a lowball rate as if he was giving that speech to a much smaller group? No way.

Even when the company came back trying to up their price by $2,000, Rashad walked away. He was not about to spend his precious time drafting a new speech for this corporation who was acting shady about using his intellectual property and rebroadcasting his speech for multiple audiences. Rashad said that if he had received the offer two years prior before joining the Speak Your Way To Cash® family, the outcome would have been much different. He would have accepted the engagement. The corporation would have given him a lowball price and probably would have *continued* to devalue his work throughout their relationship. This is the kind of strategic move that has made Rashad and other Speak Your Way To Cash® speakers so successful in their careers. They know what they are seeking in a client. If clients want to be disingenuous, these speakers have the mindset, the process, and the legal knowledge to support themselves.

Before Speak Your Way To Cash®, Rashad said he felt encouraged to take 300 engagements a year regardless of the pay or the manner in which they treated Rashad as a speaker. Now? He's limited his yearly engagements to the double digits. Instead of stressing, Rashad says that he's fishing. Just like his granddaddy, he sits back and watches what offers come into his inbox. Five figures? Travel included? Working with an industry that fuels his passion? He'll bite. A lowball price?

Having to pay for his own accommodations? He'll let it go. Rashad knows the value that he brings to the table, and he will walk away from clients who do not see or respect that value. He doesn't have to stress himself out with long negotiations and shady clients.

Corporations do have the budget to respect your intellectual property and pay you five figures to license out your creative work. Remember that. You have to protect your intellectual property and do some of the work to show that you *demand* that respect, but once you do, you can hang back and start fishing too.

Here's some things to remember from this chapter:

- You absolutely must have a solid legal strategy. You will need contracts, federally registered trademarks, and copyrights.
- Do not draft your own contracts or file your own IP documents with the federal government unless you absolutely have to (because a lawyer is out of budget).
- Make sure if you have to negotiate your own contracts you pay close attention to the IP provisions. You should seek to own your own content, so you can license it out, for a fee.

Act Your Way to Cash™

Pull out the latest contract you signed or were offered when you were booking a speaking engagement. Does this contract protect you in every "what if" situation? Will you be paid for the work that you put into each engagement even if an Act of God changes up your original plans? Don't learn the importance of contracts and force majeure clauses the hard way. Set up a legal audit with Mobile General Counsel® and allow one of the lawyers at the firm to see where you need more protection! Book this at Mobilegeneralcounsel.com/schedule-appointment.

Chapter 17

Building Your Team

When we start talking about legalities, you know things are getting serious! I have given you so much to work with in this book, and each of these big strategies comes with small tasks. Everything from building a PowerPoint to building lists of potential clients takes time. You might feel like you have a lot on your plate, but trust me, this is the path to landing six-figure contracts.

How are you going to get all of this done on your own? The answer is you don't have to do it by yourself. If you see yourself landing six-figure contracts and making a full-time career from your speaking business, you will have to hire a team to help you, or, at least, you will have to hire a person.

Who's On My Team?

Here is just a shortlist of people who I have on my team or who I have contracted for specific projects:

- Personal In-Person Assistant
- Administrator
- Backup Administrator
- Sales Assistant
- Copywriter
- Instructional Designer
- Graphic Designer
- Web Developers
- Research Associate
- Social Media Managers
- Photographer
- Videographer
- Editor (photo, copy, video, audio, etc.)
- Accountant
- Lawyer

I know what you're thinking. That is a *lot* of people (and a lot of salaries to be paid). Don't worry just yet. I'm not paying all of these people at once, and you don't have to do that either. Use this chapter as a guide to know when it's time to hire someone for your team, how to hire the right person, and what you need to share with that person to save yourself time and money.

Hiring A Team Isn't Easy

The goal of hiring a team is to save you time and money. I know that doesn't always make sense because you're paying someone along the way, but you've just had your mind blown with information on systems that can get you P.A.I.D. You can start organizing how you plan to get clients, but you don't have to be the person to implement everything. If you can hire a great team, you can collect thousands of emails, reach potential clients, and have beautiful marketing materials while you focus on more high-level tasks.

This is the goal, right? It doesn't always work that way. If you don't have the right strategy for hiring, you're going to end up with people who cost you more than their salary. This whole chapter is about to help you prevent that, but hiring can be a tricky game. I do not have it 100% figured out. This is hard stuff. Billion-dollar companies struggle to attract and retain top talent; that's why many speakers are in business! However, I will share what I know!

Here's what can happen if you aren't strategic about your hiring. A while back, I hired a woman to do sales calls for me. By this point in my career, I knew what I had to say to get a client interested in working with me. I knew how to invite clients to experience my services. I put all that down in a script. I spent weeks creating and refining this script.

I gave this script to my new hire. Her one job was to pick up the phone, dial the right numbers, and go through the script. You can guess what happened, right? She didn't go through the script. She hopped onto 50 sales calls and didn't use the script. That's a waste of over 50 hours of time! I had to go back, call the people to whom she had spoken, and make sure she was using the right script for the next 50 calls. On the first call she made with the script, she ended up closing a deal. There is no surprise there, right? I knew the script worked! It would have been easier for me to just make those first 50 sales calls on my own, but that's not what happened. When you hire people, you should have standard operating procedures or step-by-step guides that show them how to do their job (SOPs is another term for this), but you also need to do quality checks. You need a process to check your people's work. If you don't, they will not follow those pretty processes you have in place. That's where I messed up. I did not check that she was following the procedures we have in place. My fault. Lesson learned.

Was that as bad as the time an assistant erased everything on my website on their first day on the job? Maybe. (Yes, that happened too.) I'm going to be honest with you before we really get into the good stuff. I told you I would keep it real. There are risks to hiring. Not everyone who I've hired has been the right person for the job. I've let people go, but it was not a waste of money or time because every time I hire, I learn, and I refine my process. If anyone reading this book has the secrets to hiring the right person for the job every time, please shoot me an email. We haven't cracked the code, but we have found ways to reduce stress and avoid situations like the one I just shared. We've hired some awesome folks too. One admin helped us land over

15 podcast features. Another admin helped me close a $150,000 contract. Another person helped us land over $60,000 in contracts and referrals. I can trace some opportunities directly back to hiring and training the right team members. If you are strategic about your hiring, you will find people who can help you implement your vision and grow your business beyond what you could do alone.

Check Your Beliefs

Are you ready to hire? If you believe that your vision is more than you can implement yourself, you have to hire some help.

Some speakers feel that they are not ready to hire. They believe it's too expensive. Here's the truth. It is hard to lead your company's growth and do all the tasks in your business at the same time. There aren't enough hours in a day to set up and implement everything we have covered in this book. That said, hiring isn't without drawbacks, and you will have to spend time training your team. However, you're not reading this book because you want a quick, easy, or *small* speaking career. If you want to build a business that deals with six-figure contracts, you have to have some help.

Check yourself at this moment. The question isn't, *Do I want to hire a team?* The question is, *Does my vision require me to hire a team?* If you've made it this far in the book, the answer probably is yes. Let's talk about what you need in place before hiring your team.

Your First Steps

Here's what I did before I made my first few hires. I got my mind right, first and foremost. I made sure that I had a strong vision. I also had my trademarks, copyrights, and other legalities in order before I hired someone. Hiring is about finding someone to carry out the strategies that you have created for your business. Before you can give someone a task, you need to know what tasks need to be done.

At this point in your career, you may have a handful of tasks that you want to delegate to contractors or an employee. Once you have these tasks in mind, it's time to check your budget. How much can you spare a month? $10 an hour? $20 an hour? $6 an hour? Rates for positions like a virtual assistant or a graphic designer can range from $5-$75+ per hour depending on where you hire them.

That's right—$5. Websites like OnlineJobs.Ph, Upwork.com, or Fiverr.com make it easy to find an international contractor for extremely reasonable rates. Of course, there are going to be some things to consider before you hire someone at that price. People who work for lower rates often require more training and direction. They also may have less loyalty to you because they are seeking other clients to make ends meet. I don't blame a virtual assistant who gets up and leaves me for someone paying twice the rate. When I find a contractor who I like, I let that person tell me what rates they are being offered, so I can match them (or pay more).

You can find people who you like at any rate. A budget is not what makes an administrator or a graphic designer a great hire. It's that person's character and skill set. I hire people for their resourcefulness, talent, motivation, and drive. You can find someone who fits that criteria and only charges $5 an hour. You also can find someone who *doesn't* fit that criteria and refuses to work for less than $40 an hour. Focus on what *you* can afford first. Do not get caught up! You need someone who is reliable, has great reviews, and can do the work. We will talk about weeding people out in a bit, but first, let's discuss how to get the most bang for your buck when you are hiring.

Let me be clear. The skill set is more important than the rate. For instance, my copywriter is excellent, and copywriting is critically important. His rate is more than $100 per hour, but he's great, and I have him on retainer. Also, writing is a skill and a gift. You may need to budget more for that. On the other hand, I have a researcher who charges me per project, and it's a smaller flat fee. They have a database from which they pull the research, so it's not particularly customized, and it doesn't take them a long time. Therefore, they are affordable. I contrast all of this with coaches. I spent more than $150,000 in professional development last year alone for experts who will come in and give me ideas. I pay a premium every time because they have the propensity to expand my vision.

When you think about what you will pay for what you want, you need a clear view of the return. Great copy sells. What I mean is this. The words on my website either can lead people to want to pay for my services or repel them, so I need to hire a great copywriter. I pay more for that. Coaches teach me skills I will have for life. I pay more for that. If you are doing admin work or research, it is important, but you are not going to change the vision of the company. I pay for it, but it is categorically different. Be reasonable when assessing what you will and won't pay for.

Hire One Person For One Job

Here's my best tip for hiring someone who will stick around and be worth your money. Hire one person to do one thing. You have a specific craft that you have built over years. If you had to pivot suddenly and take up graphic design, photography, or another skill in which you have no training, you wouldn't be able to produce high-quality work. Apply that same idea to your team. Your copywriter is not going to do a better job at graphics than a graphic designer. A research associate doesn't always make a great instructional designer. Find someone who goes by the title of what you are seeking, and hire that person to do one job only. Do not waste time waiting for your graphic designer to become trained in copywriting or for your photographer to become trained in graphic design.

There are so many copywriters, virtual assistants, or instructional designers out there just waiting for you to hire them. Where do you start? The answer depends on what tasks you have in your strategy and where you would like to save time. Do you find yourself struggling on Canva to create PowerPoints for your presentations? Start with a designer. Do you need to put together a speaking reel? An editor or a videographer can help you out with that. There are plenty of freelancers *and* potential employees out there who can fill any of these positions.

Don't hire them all at once. Remember, you build a team that can carry out your vision. If that vision includes scheduling a lot of calls with potential clients, a virtual assistant or administrator may be the best person to hire. If you need to *find* potential clients first, a social media manager or market researcher may be the better hire. Go through your strategies and see where someone can fill in the gaps and take tasks off your hands.

Weed Them Out

I'm making sure to drop *all* the gems in this chapter because hiring is hard, and I'm putting that nicely. Hiring is the hardest thing I've had to do as a business owner, and I'm also putting *that* nicely. I had an accountant tell me once that I had to be prepared to invest 90 days with a new hire with no return on investment (ROI). That's three months. That's a lot of time to be holding someone's hand.

To cut down on those 90 days, I have an extensive testing process for new hires. The application is not something you can finish in a few minutes. If someone is determined to work for me, that person will fill it out. People who are turned off by the length of the application are probably people who I don't want to hire in the first place. People who ask me dozens of questions about the application are probably people who I don't want to hire either, and that's okay! Weeding out applicants is a good thing. I don't want to waste my precious time looking through resumes or applications. This is for a full-time administrative position. Every position requires a different process. I ask a lot of questions in this written interview such as:

1. How would you describe what we do at Speak Your Way To Cash®?

2. Who are our clients from what you can gather?

3. If you get an email stating X from a client, what email would you send the client? What email would you send to me?

Most of the questions allow me to see how the potential hire thinks and communicates. Also, I ask questions with answers that the potential hire could find with a quick Google search. The truth is when you run a small company, you can't hold their hands a lot. You need self-starters. You have to test for that.

Once the potential hire gets past the testing process, I hold interviews and a trial period. I want to know if the potential hire is a critical thinker, so I throw different scenarios at them along the way. What do they do if a client can't find their login information? How would they fix a presentation based on my feedback? If they don't know how to handle basic situations, I will know quickly that it's not a good fit.

Training

Training doesn't end after the trial period is over. I've got a whole *system* and a workflow set up when someone new is added to the team. They get all of the proper new hire paperwork, non-disclosure agreements, and other key documents. Even with an automated system that sends out paperwork or applications, I have to spend some time training my team, offering feedback, and giving further instruction for larger tasks down the road.

I have entire courses set up on Kartra for my team to watch during training. I record videos on Loom to walk my team through each step of what I need them to do. Every person who works with me gets feedback constantly from me about how to align their work with my vision for my companies. I know that management may not be the reason you got into entrepreneurship, but it's a *big* part of it. Don't sleep on it.

If you're paying lower hourly rates, expect to conduct more training. People you hire outside of your home country may require training about doing business in your country. That's okay because the right person will take that training and apply it to everything they do. You will need to know how to do business with them too. Learn about the culture of your team members including contractors and employees. Team building and making sure everyone feels safe and secure is a big part of what Chris does at our company. He's awesome at it! Be prepared to train your team. They might know *nothing* about your brand before they start working for you, and now they have to be a *representative* of your brand. You have to educate them on how you do business, how you talk to customers, and what you expect of them. If you can communicate this from the start, you will reduce your risk of spending 90 days paying someone who is not a good fit.

In a perfect world, the first person you hire will be able to stick with you forever and do the best work they can do for your business. That doesn't always happen. Contractors find other jobs. People go on leave, and your team will expand as your business expands. As you start training your team, you will see the systems that you need to put in place as you bring on new people or replace current contractors. Developing a hiring process takes time. I'm not going to tell you that you can rush through the hiring process because, in reality, you just can't. All you can do is be strategic, plan appropriately, and recognize where you need people to help you carry out your vision.

Do I find myself with more stress than relief when I bring on a new hire? Sometimes, I do. Do I wish that I could handle every single task myself? If I had 48 hours in a day, maybe I would. Would I be able to grow as fast as I am without a team to carry out my vision? Absolutely not. I can't do all the tasks that I need to do. I don't *want* to do all of the tasks that I need to do. Twelve-hour days of mundane tasks won't fill your cup. You started this business because you want to share your gifts. Give your contractors the chance to do the same but in a way that helps you out.

In an ideal world, I would have hired an HR recruiter to handle all of my hires from the beginning. Not every speaker has access to that type of budget, but building a strong team and being strategic about hiring will get you there. I'm not telling you to go out and hire a team today, but once you get your systems rolling and start building momentum, revisit this chapter. Your freelancers and your team are hired to carry out the systems you have put in place. They carry out your vision. This whole process begins with you, your gifts, and the transformation you want to see in your clients, and that's what you're doing right now!

Meet Maria Davis-Pierre

Maria Davis-Pierre knows a little something about being busy. Maria is the CEO of Autism in Black, a business that provides advocacy, education, and support to Black parents of children who are on the autism spectrum. She offers coaching sessions, training, and she delivers speeches around the country. She also hosted the first ever Autism in Black Conference in 2021.

As the founder of one of the few organizations working in this space, Maria receives a lot of requests to speak to the press. She has been featured in *Forbes Magazine*, *USA Today*, and *The New York Times*. All this was happening before she joined the Speak Your Way To Cash® Facebook group and attended our conference back in October 2020. However, as she became involved in the community, she started to see how she could use these features strategically as a way to share her value with potential clients and land five-figure speaking contracts.

When she was quoted in *USA Today* and gave her opinion on a controversial movie in the autism community, she posted the link in the Speak Your Way To Cash® Facebook group. I told her congratulations, and then I told her that this was a big opportunity. Maria needed to tell all of her potential clients about this feature, so they could then see what she was doing. That's what she did! She put the *USA Today* feature in her email signature, on her newsletter, and throughout her marketing materials. Can you guess what happened when she did that?

She got the opportunity from an international news platform to talk about her thoughts concerning the movie. Now, she has even more information to share with her potential clients.

You might be asking me why I'm telling you this story right here. We already talked about landing press features a few chapters ago! However, Maria's success isn't just about how she shared her feature in *USA Today*. This got the wheels turning. She saw the importance of repurposing and using content strategically in order to reach potential clients. A quote in *USA Today* became content for her newsletter or social media platforms. What other content could she repurpose and use to make her life easier and her business more visible?

Here is what she does now. Maria records The Autism in Black podcast every week. Each week has a new theme. Then, she repurposes that content and creates a YouTube video and a blog post based on that podcast. Everything is centered around that same topic, and she is able to reach more people through multiple forms of media.

What does Maria do during this process? She sits down to record the podcast, and her team does the rest. Yes, she's got a team. Her two virtual assistants (VAs) do all of her content writing, podcast editing, and social media content creation. In the future, she plans to hire someone who can do research on conferences and clients whom she can contact for even *more* engagements and partnerships.

Hiring VAs comes with challenges. Maria's brand is very important to her, so she needs a team that understands where she is coming from and how to approach content writing in her voice. Luckily, her main VA is a therapist herself, but Maria still took two months to train her in order to let her take the reins in her content creation strategy.

Maria sees outsourcing tasks to VAs as a form of self-care. Remember, this woman is *busy* creating resources, speaking to families, and training colleges and corporations. Through Speak Your Way To Cash®, she has been able to see the benefit in building out a team strategically and developing a strong content creation strategy that requires little work from her. This approach already is producing results. By March 2021, Maria was booked out through the rest of the year!

Below are some key takeaways from this chapter:

- When considering if you can afford to hire, leverage the international marketplace.

- Be sure to have a hiring process in place before you hire, so you can ensure you are working with the right people.

- Do not avoid hiring your team members and being clear about the tasks you want them to complete.

- Hire one person to do one thing and make sure you have SOPs for them to follow and a process to check and see if they actually are following your procedures.

Act Your Way to Cash™

Look at your strategies and to-do lists. Is there one task that you can delegate to someone? Maybe your proposal needs a bolder design. Maybe your website copy isn't cutting it. A one-off project can help you dip your toes into the hiring and contracting pool. Take those first steps to determine who you are seeking, what rates you are willing to pay, and what systems you need to put in place as you grow your team and make more hiring decisions in the future.

If you are not sure where to start hiring, these websites and resources are your best bet:

- Upwork

- Fiverr

- Indeed

- Connections with friends and family

- Alumni networks

Personally, I like Fiverr, but entrepreneurs have great experiences finding help through other means. You may be surprised at the rates at which you can get high-quality contractors for small, medium, and large tasks. You also can ask for recommendations in the Speak Your Way To Cash® Facebook group. The right contractor for you may be currently working with another speaker in the group right now!

Chapter 18

Bringing It All Together: Deciding Your Next Steps

When I landed my first large contract, it was valued at $60,000. To me, that was a large contract. I was so excited. I thought about all the people who had told me "no" previously, and I realized something; it took me the same energy to get a $60,000 contract as it did to get a $5,000 contract. That changed everything for me. I started being deliberate about who I was pitching, how I was pitching them, and what they would see when they looked me up online. After just a few weeks of focused effort, I landed three additional $60,000 contracts. Then, I landed a $180,000 contract. Then, I landed another contract and another contract! It kept going up from there. It was no harder running a business fueled by larger contracts than it was running one fueled by lower-paying clients. That's why I created The P.A.I.D. Method™ for speakers and consultants because for the most part, the messages to us are clear. Work your way from the bottom up, and when you reach the top, be glad. The P.A.I.D. Method™ flips that notion on its head. I believe that you can start at the top of the speaking market versus working your way up from the bottom, and I am hoping this book will help you do just that.

An Overview Of What We Learned

I want to recap what we have covered, so you can be clear about how to implement the information in this book.

In Part One, we discussed mindset. You absolutely have to get your mind right before you do anything else. If you don't police your negative thoughts, they will turn into negative beliefs. Those beliefs will halt any positive actions you try to take. You can't just believe that six-figure contracts are out there. You have to believe that they are out there *for you*.

Next, in Chapter 3, we covered how you can use the F.A.M.E. Method™ to choose your topic and audience and develop your proprietary framework. A solid speaking career demands that you know to whom you are talking and how you will solve their problems. After you have your topic, audience, and framework, you are ready to build your brand with the press!

In Part Two, we covered several ways you can leverage the press to build your speaking brand, and we covered a few of them. We discussed owned media, earned media, and paid media! Owned media simply describes your social media content, blogs you write, and other content that you create. Earned media describes media features on other people's platforms (podcasts, news features, etc.). Paid media describes media opportunities that you pay for. Paid ads are a good example of paid media. You want to make sure when potential clients Google you, the right material comes up!

Next, in Part Three, we discussed assembling your offer. This was a biggie. We covered elements of your six-figure proposal and pricing! Pricing will be informed by your market research so don't skip this part of the process! We covered a number of items that you can include in your six-figure proposal such as consulting, workshops, on-demand training programs, and more.

Then, in Part Four, we discussed sales. We covered how you effectively can invite people to work with you. Selling is a critical element to any business. In this book, we dove into the exact questions you need to include in your sales script to close more deals! I hope you took notes during that discussion! We described how you could get more clients by hosting virtual events for your ideal customers to attend. You need a crystal clear view of who your ideal client is in order for this strategy to work. Specifically, you need a list of the job titles of all the people who could hire you potentially. This list will be really helpful when you are gathering the contact information for people to whom you can pitch. Next, you need to put together a hot list of potential clients. After you have that list, you have to reach out to them. Don't ask them to work with you. *Invite them* to an event that you put together to help them. It's always about the client. That's the difference between purely pitching with no invite strategy and inviting people to work with you. Our methods are client-centric.

What happens after you land a client? In Part Five, we covered what happens after you land a client. We illustrated how you can put together a customer map and what should be included in your client acquisition process. It is no secret that you need to deliver impactful tasks for clients. So, we discussed strategies you can use to keep clients engaged - both virtually and in-person. After you do a great job for your clients, we gave you a script you can use to ask them for referrals! Did you miss that part? Read the section on delivery again! It covers customer service and techniques for crushing your talk!

To end it all, in Part Six, we covered scaling your speaking business with a solid legal and hiring strategy! We covered why it's critical that you have contracts, copyrights and trademarks in your business. Notably, you learned how having a solid legal strategy can help you generate more revenue in your business. Recall our discussion on licensing. Protect your intellectual property. It's very valuable.

Whew!

We went through a lot of information in one book, and you may be thinking, Okay, this was cool, but I want more guidance in implementing all of this stuff.

Who can help me with this?

I am glad you asked.

If you want to implement The P.A.I.D. Method™ with me and a group of other accomplished speakers and professionals just like you, apply to work with me in my group coaching program. My program has three parts:

1. Group Coaching. I will coach you live in a group setting and answer questions you have about growing your speaking practice. These sessions take place virtually, and I help speakers around the world to implement these methods.

2. Community. You will be cheered on, advised, and supported by a group of speakers going through the same process as you, and the support from our community is unmatched. We have a private group where members of our community can network and seek guidance from one another.

3. On-demand learning and guidance that you can access 24/7 from anywhere in the world (with access to the internet). I personally recorded over 10+ hours of content and had it edited down into modules that are aimed at guiding you through the process of building out your six-figure speaking proposal.

Here's a sneak peek of what students in my private group coaching program receive.

- Group coaching calls. They are valued at more than $30,000.

- 10+hours of pre-recorded bonus trainings and additional sessions. They are valued at more than $15,000.

- 60+ activities, handouts, templates, SOPs, and more created by my team and I. They are valued at more than $50,000.

- A private community from which you can glean and learn information daily. Our community is invaluable.

This program is the best program for speakers looking to implement the P.A.I.D. Method™. I spent more than one year doing market research and working with the best instructional designers to make it happen. We have had students land their first five and first six-figure contracts after joining! Check out the Speak Your Way To Cash® Podcast Episode entitled, *How SYWTC Academy Student Dorianne Landed Her First Six-Figure Speaking Contract & How You Can Too!* In that episode, Dorianne breaks down her biggest money and mindset wins since joining the Academy! She achieved this result in less than one year, and she's not the only success story!

Are you interested? Apply at *www.speakyourwaytocash.com/apply*

Implement!

Even if you don't work with me, I hope that you walk away from this book with a plan for implementing the strategies I shared with you. This book has a lot of information. You don't have to do everything, every day. As you get to the final pages of this book, I urge you to develop an implementation strategy. How many invitations can you send out per week? How many people can you connect with today? What package can you offer your clients?

If you want to see results, you need focus. You need tunnel vision. Now is your time to *commit* to walking through that tunnel without making any pit stops. Yes, you'll have to say "no" to engagements that do not help you achieve your goals. Yes, you will have to walk away from opportunities that might otherwise look tempting. Yes, you'll have to put some of your feelings aside when you say "no" to things. We all have to do it. Not everything that comes your way is going to serve you. That free speaking engagement probably is not going to serve you. The lowball offer at a corporation that comes with an NDA and miles of red tape is not serving you. You've read about speakers like Rashad Rayford who walked away from offers that undervalued his gifts. Can you guess what happened? His career was much better because he made that decision. From the moment you put down this book, you have to commit to yourself to do only what serves you and your business.

That's what tunnel vision is about, and it's how six-figure speakers become seven-figure speakers. A lot of us have different people pulling us in every which way: partners, friends, family, colleagues, even coaches. I know speakers who have 7 different coaches telling them to go in 7 different directions. That's not serving anyone. Step away from the people who aren't aligned with your vision. Work with coaches who are pushing you in the right direction. Keep that tunnel vision *tight*.

Put In the Work!

If you ran into me on the street tomorrow and told me that you read my book, I would ask you how you are implementing the strategies taught here. Why? I can tell from people's actions whether they truly want something. The activities in which you are investing your time tell me everything I need to know about where you want to go and if you're going to get there. What you truly want, you take action to achieve.

I know I have touched on this a few times, but I've got to say this again before I let you walk down this path toward your elevated speaking career. Getting the results you want for your business is going to take time. The first invitation you send to a client may not turn into a six-figure contract. That's okay. That's the name of the game. I tell all my speaking clients to give themselves three months of consistent activities before they start expecting results. I'm not even talking about "results" like six-figure contracts. Give yourself three months before you start scheduling calls with potential clients.

Six-figure speaking contracts don't appear magically on your doorstep overnight. The average speaker is in the game for 10 years before they reach seven figures. The average speaker also is not making six figures right now. That doesn't mean you can't make six figures. The success my clients have reached through The P.A.I.D. Method™ tells me that you can. However, you can't make six figures until you start putting in the work consistently. Thirty pitches one week and none for the next three weeks isn't going to cut it. Remember, I sent out 300 pitches *a week* consistently to book 25 engagements on my first speaking tour. I should note that the better you target and narrow down your audience, the less people you will need to pitch, but that too takes time. That won't happen over the course of one week. Keep at it. Plan to implement your strategy for up to a year before booking that six-figure speaking contract. I know that once you do, you'll thank me.

Let's Keep in Touch.

I know you're probably hyped up about finishing this book and taking some big steps in your speaking career, but this book is just a small *piece* of what you can learn with Speak Your Way To Cash®. If you are excited to hear more gems and keep working on your speaking business, there are a few ways that you can reach me:

- Join the free Speak Your Way To Cash® Facebook group (if you haven't already) and ask a question in the group about the next steps you need to take to elevate your speaking career.

- Subscribe to the Speak Your Way To Cash® podcast and listen to coaching episodes, solo episodes, and interviews with some of the speakers you heard about in this book.

- Apply to join my group coaching program, the Speak Your Way To Cash® Academy, if you want to land five to six-figure corporate speaking contracts.

- Enroll in the Speak Your Way To Cash® course if you want to get started in the college market.

Do you want to explore more options and continue this conversation? Send an email to ashley@speakyourwaytocash.com with "Work With Speak Your Way To Cash®" as the subject line or learn more at speakyourwaytocash.com.

That's all she wrote! (Well, not everything.) Congratulations on finishing this book. You have joined many speakers who are using The P.A.I.D. Method™ to land large speaking contracts. You should be proud of yourself! I can't wait to see the ways that you implement what you have learned.

Speak Your Way To Cash® Resources

To access more information on any of the resources below, go to www.speakyourwaytocash.com.

Speak Your Way to Cash® Facebook Group

A Facebook group featuring live videos and content aimed at helping speakers advance their speaking careers. It is perfect for those who desire community without the financial commitment. This is not a coaching community, but rather a member-led free Facebook community.

Speak Your Way to Cash® Podcast

In this dynamic series, Ashley shares business tactics, tips, and strategies from her own experience in both law and business. She also interviews experts in the speaking, sales, and entrepreneurship spaces to examine their successes and pitfalls. It is ideal for speakers who want to listen to the journey of how six, seven, and eight-figure speakers have amplified their brands using the power of speaking. It's available on most major podcast streaming platforms.

Paid Offerings:

Speak Your Way to Cash® Course

A completely self-paced course that teaches people how to book one-off speaking engagements with colleges and companies. It includes aids such as scripts and swipe copies. It is an entry-level course ideal for speakers who are not ready to form their 5 to six-figure proposals but are looking to land smaller, one-time engagements. We do not cover how to assemble or pitch large corporate contracts in this course.

Speak Your Way to Cash® Academy

A group coaching program that provides speakers with the tools needed to book five to six-figure corporate speaking contracts. It is perfect for speakers who are ready to build six-figure proposals. Members have access to SOPs, handouts, templates, and live coaching sessions to guide them in pitching their speaking services to corporate and collegiate clients.

Event Offerings:

Speak Your Way to Cash® Live Event

The #1 event for speakers seeking to land larger corporate speaking engagements and consulting contracts. This interactive coaching event features a culmination of Ashley's business expertise and speaking prowess. Participants will Mastermind with Ashley about strategies to automate their businesses and hear testimonials from past and current clients. They also will walk away with actionable knowledge about how to pitch and ultimately land five to six-figure contracts, manage referrals, and expand their brands.

One-On-One Services:

Speak Your Way to Cash® One-On-One Strategy Experience

An intensive 4-hour, 1-on-1 virtual session with Ashley to help speakers jumpstart their careers and take them to the next level. This experience is an amazing opportunity to develop personalized press, pitch, and speaker sales plans with an expert who has helped speakers land paid engagements all over the world. This premium investment is designed for the busy speakers who are otherwise engaged and are looking to mastermind strategies about building out their personal sales plan for corporations one-on-one with Ashley or a member of her personal coaching team.

For more information, go to www.speakyourwaytocash.com.

Notes

Introduction

1. Grand View Research. (2021). *Virtual events market size, share & trends analysis report by event type, by service, by establishment size, by end-use, by application, by industry vertical, by use-case, by region, and segment forecasts, 2021 - 2028.* Grand View Research. https://www.grandviewresearch.com/industry-analysis/virtual-events-market

Chapter 1: Developing the Mindset of a Highly Paid Speaker

2. Alton, L. (2018). *Why low self-esteem may be hurting you at work.* NBC News. https://www.nbcnews.com/better/business/why-low-self-esteem-may-be-hurting-your-career-ncna814156#:%7E:text=3%20Tips%20for%20Improving%20Your,a%20happy%20and%20lucrative%20career.

Chapter 5: Scoring Clients with Social Media and Owned Media

3. Facebook IQ. (2019). *Facebook IQ: How Instagram boosts brands and drives sales.* Facebook for Business. https://www.facebook.com/unsupportedbrowser

4. Schomer, A. (2019). *LinkedIn, Pinterest, Instagram most trusted platforms; Facebook least.* Business Insider. https://www.businessinsider.com/linkedin-pinterest-instagram-top-spots-2019-digital-trust-report-facebook-stays-last?international=true&r=US&IR=T

Chapter 15: Delivering a Great Customer Experience

1. Gallo, A. (2014). *The value of keeping the right customers.* Harvard Business Review.
   https://hbr.org/2014/10/the-value-of-keeping-the-right-customers

2. *Customer Retention Should Outweigh Customer Acquisition.* RESCI.
   https://www.retentionscience.com/blog/customer-retention-should-out-weigh-customer-acquisition/

3. Slough, A. (2020). *I see you! How technology increases customer transparency and lifetime value.* Forrester.
   https://go.forrester.com/blogs/i-see-you-how-technology-increases-customer-transparency-and-lifetime-value/

4. *40 Customer Retention Statistics You Need to Know.* GetFeedback.
   https://www.getfeedback.com/resources/cx/40-stats-churn-customer-satisfaction/

About Ashley Nicole Kirkwood

Ashley Nicole Kirkwood has many titles: entrepreneur, lawyer, wife, and mom, but professionally, what excites her most is being known as a skilled presenter and valued teacher.

Not many people would leave a "safe" job as a corporate attorney to start their own firm, but Ashley did it, and she has experienced exceptional success. After she started her own firm, she discovered her true calling—speaking. She knew she had a lot to offer, but she started getting small paid gigs. She quickly grew frustrated with the "accepted roadmap" to a speaking career (grind it out for years of low-paying gigs). No, no, no…

Ashley got to work and cracked the code. By sheer will and talent, she discovered it's not a matter of making a name for yourself over time. A successful speaking career is about presenting yourself the right way to the right people in the right organizations. The big money gigs started piling up.

Ashley then took it a step further and began Speak Your Way To Cash®, which has grown to be one of the leading speaker training organizations in the world. The book you are holding is the literary version of this industry-busting brand.

There's room for you in this billion dollar speaking industry, and Speak Your Way To Cash® is your ticket in.

Ready to skyrocket your
speaking career?

Are you an entrepreneur or speaker without a trademark, federal copyright, or contract?

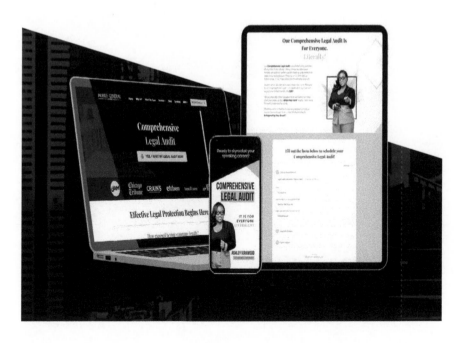